The Other Side of the Hedge

by

Paul Martin

Illustrated by

Phillip Hamenioux

Forward

This book, the memoirs of the late Paul Martin, has been published many years after it was written by him, in memory of a true country lad who was always at one with nature.

In later years he turned away from hunting and concentrated on his love of birds of prey, eventually opening Haven Falconry Bird of Prey Centre on the Isle of Wight in 2016

He was a great mentor in his later years, passing his boundless knowledge of all thing's country and wildlife to all those who showed an interest.

He is greatly missed by many.

I dedicate this book to my Mother and Father for putting up with my endless antics as a youngster. To my wife and children for the times I should have been at home with them but was out walking with the dogs instead, and to everyone involved in helping me put this book together.

Very special thanks the hugely talented illustrator.

Right from a very early age I found myself gazing with utter curiosity at anything and everything – fish, fur and feather, that moved. As the years have gone on I have become even more interested in such things and although most of my time in the field has been spent hunting, it is also good to sit back once in a while and just observe. To me there is no better form of relaxation. When one really stops to think about it, we are all very fortunate in the fact that we can watch all the beauty around us from

The other side of the hedge.

Megs First Encounter With Reynard

A mild windy night, full moon and very light, so light it was casting a shadow as I walked. A local butcher had an ordered ten rabbits, I didn't know whether I could fulfil it because of the state of the night, plus both my dogs are not very fit. My best dog Belle had just had a very healthy litter of pups, ten in all, hence her lack of fitness. I have kept one pup for myself, she looks good but time will tell. My second dog Meg is only fifteen months old, still a puppy really, inexperienced and six weeks previously had a bad time with a barbed-wire fence, causing her to have quite a few stitches. Before her mishap, she was coming on quite well, picking up rabbits and hares and showing keen interest in foxes, although not had one yet, but she will I feel sure.

This night I was going to a good range of fields that I looked at a few evenings ago. I saw rabbits out feeding so hopefully, they will be there now. Haven't lamped there before, so I don't know who might be about. I parked the car some half a mile from the fields, put both dogs on their leads, lamp over my shoulder and off we went.

Looking down I can see both dogs quivering with excitement. I approach the first gate and climb over, call the dogs and both come over the top. Now I walk along the hedgerow and get myself in a good position, switch on the beam. Already I see a few squatters and a few running around further up the field. Off the slip went Meg. A squatter moves slightly as the beam found it. Straight in Meg went and neatly picks it up after a very short run.

Another rabbit has heard the commotion and makes a fast run for it. Belle sees it and I let her go. The rabbit makes it to the hedge, it is nearly lost, but Belle turns it. The rabbit makes a fatal mistake and heads back up the field; Belle gains ground and strikes. A well caught rabbit is returned to hand by both dogs, still live and unspoilt. On we go and another three rabbits were caught in that field.

The next field is somewhat more awkward as I am blessed with the farmer deciding to put his young Heifer calves on it, for grazing. They are a bloody nuisance! So inquisitive and noisy. I fear for my dogs as a good kick would certainly put a dog out of action, if not worse, for some time. Again, I walk along the hedgerow, lamp off so hopefully the calves won't see where I am. I am halfway across the field; maybe just one quick flash with the lamp. Hello what's that, thunder? No, it's those bloody calves running towards me.......I'm off!

The next field is better than the last. Well it couldn't be much worse could it? The dogs catch me another three and just as I am having a last look, I spy those two round glaring eyes of Reynard, both dogs have seen him as well. I let both dogs go in pursuit, knowing Belle is just going to have a look, but Meg may do better. I see as predicted Belle stop short, but Meg goes on. The fox, not seemingly to be in a hurry, but aware something is amiss. Meg draws in the gap until she is feet away from Reynard's backside, and bang she strikes. I see Reynard fall, but recover and go on his way. Meg returns to me totally bewildered. I tell her she has done well, she wags her tail, and we go on, maybe next time she will hold a fox.

We go back to the car and deposit the rabbits we have, and cross the road to some other fields. I end up going to the long way around – cows remember!

Rabbits safely back and over into a newly sown field just opposite to the car. In the field are a few hares which sit bolt upright on detecting the beam. I decide to leave them and go for some easy rabbits in the middle. On a light moonlit night like this, you would not expect to see rabbits out so far (so the books say). This was the field that I made up my order for ten rabbits and pleased with catch, I head back to the car.

I paunched the night's bag, stand and have a cigarette, and just marvel at this beautiful world, which is even better at night. A really good place to lamp is this, I think I'll come here again. Anyway, off home now, there's work in the morning, I'll have that fox next time, you see!

A Lucky Catch

I decided to go out earlier than usual for just a quick flick round some of the fields not far from home. The night was quite overcast, so no moon showing, just a light breeze and darkness. The turn out of rabbits was very poor indeed, the whole evening only showed about fifteen all told. But hares seemed many. So as the purpose of the night was simply to give the dogs a run and enjoy myself, it made no difference as to the type of quarry.

There seem to be two type of true lurcher men to me, those who go for rabbits, with anything else which they are fortunate to get, and those who go solely for hares. I feel that with the dogs I have, I am not one of the latter.

My smallest bitch stands 23 ½", with a Bedlington Collie/Greyhound parentage, and is a most powerful dog, with stamina to run all night long and more. But she is no hare catcher. However, she has an uncanny amount of hunting instinct, and is beautiful to watch lamping rabbits, done with such apparent ease – it is breath-taking. I have been out with quite a selection of lamping mates and each one that has seen this bitch work has been totally astounded as to her skill.

My second dog (Meg) is Bedlington/Greyhound and Greyhound Collie parentage, standing at 25", and as mentioned before, is still a pup at 15 months old. She is very fast day at night if using a lamp, you can literally see her closing into her quarry. The problem being with the majority of young dogs, is, they appear to be oblivious of the fact that Quarry can turn on a sixpence and therefore miss and overshoot. By the time ground is made up the rabbit or hare is far enough away to make his escape. I have found that as young dogs become mature and experienced, they tend to get crafty and calculate the habits and movements of quarry – and then success is found.

Going on with my story – in no time at all I came across a hare, I approached it as silently as possibly to about thirty yards. When he then broke cover and headed to the nearest hedge, the dogs were sent on course. Meg was some five yards in front of Belle turning the hare back and forth. Belle seems to know that if she hangs back the hare will eventually come within striking distance, and sure enough the hare makes a fatal mistake by out-turning Meg – right into Belle's path, Belle strikes and the hare is ours.

I recall the first time I saw a dog pursue a rabbit, it was some years ago, but the feeling and sight were incredible My adrenalin was pumping and the whole event was absolute magic. Everything I see or catch, even to this day is still the same. The Magic has never faded. And there are so many other bonuses too – the friendship I have with my dogs, it is a three-way partnership that cannot be broken as we all enjoy each other's' company. The freedom that I enjoy of just being alone, somehow, I can work out all my day to day problems by just walking and hunting with my dogs. I find an Inner Peace within that I cannot find anywhere else. And when I return home after being out for a few hours, I am totally happy with my life and lot.

By being out at such strange time of night, it is amazing what one can see. Normal people, for want of a better expression, seem to miss out so much. I see foxes, badgers, owls, deer and a whole host of things. I always think that their lives must be very dull. If only they knew what they were missing.

The evening went on, not much to write home about I am afraid, but I had good fun, and some good courses on both hare and rabbit. Two hares and a few rabbits were caught in all.

Retrieving A Fox

An old friend of mine turned up at about 9pm, he asked if I fancied some lamping.

'Why not?' I replied. 'So let's go over to the golf course.'

The night was breezy, reasonably dark and dry. On our arrival we spotted a fair few squatting rabbits. My mate had brought his two dogs, one of them a Deerhound/Greyhound Cross and the other a Greyhound/ Whippet. The latter, incidentally, was the dog I recently bred with Belle.

The Deerhound Greyhound Cross is now about six years old, and I understand has been a handy dog in his day. Sadly, he is slowing down somewhat these days, but can still give a hare or fox a good run for his money.

A few weeks ago, my mate and I were out with our dogs, when he spotted a fox in the lamp beam Jim – my mate, sent his dog on – he was off as quick as a flash. The chase seemed to go on and on, only to disappear out of sight. We waited about then to fifteen minutes, still no dog, so we went to look for him. As we approached the field and shone the beam, it revealed the dog standing in the middle of the field with a large dog fox in his mouth. It must have taken another twenty minutes or so to get the fox from him. This dog is a renowned fox killer and seems to enjoy every minute of it.

Jim's other dog – Greyhound Whippet is about three years old and has been an extremely fast dog. Alas, I think, he has run too hard and fast as a pup, and now has three or four broken toes. He still manages to catch a few rabbits and hares, but nothing like he should be capable of.

We had a good time on the golf course and got sixteen rabbits between us. It is quite amazing how much faster a rabbit can run on short, well-tended grass, such as a golf course. They seem to know exactly where to run in an instant, I think that rabbits that are run and caught by a dog on such ground are very well earned.

Reference the amount of rabbits that I catch, I know for some of you maybe thinking that the catches are really quite small, and indeed you're right. But you see, I live on the Isle of Wight, which you can appreciate is a small place, with an extremely large population of Lurcher owners. This of course means that nearly every field is lamped about two or three times a week, and we are already breaking the back of the rabbit population. However, in winter months, I tend to spend as much time as possible on the mainland, where game is much more plentiful.

On the Island we have no wild deer, so to go to the Mainland is a treat indeed. There are so many unlamped areas, that us Islanders get rather spoilt. I bring back quite a good bag from the Mainland usually, as I will report to you further on in this book.

Too Fast Too Soon

Some six months ago, a friend and I had a most distressing time whilst we were lamping.

We left home at about 10.30pm on a night and went to some fields that are quite local to where we live. The night was good, dark, windy and quite cool. There were good amount of rabbits and hares about, so we were assured of a good few runs.

We had two dogs each, me with my two, (I have already given details of their breeds) and my mate, with his Deerhound Greyhound cross and his young dog was (Pip) a Deerhound/Greyhound Saluki. This dog was a fine-looking specimen, with great stamina, and appeared to have plenty of staying power. Pip and my dog Meg, were the same age, about thirteen months old. So, because of their young age we intended not to run them too hard. But as I have said, there was plenty to be caught.

We were so into our lamping, so to speak, that we completely lost all track of time and before we knew it, it was about 2.30am. Having had an extremely good night and covered a fair amount of ground we decided to call it a night. Setting off for home we had to pass a large field where hares usually sit. I shone the beam across the hedge to see a hare in the middle. As the say goes: 'it seemed a good idea at the time' – to let all four dogs go for a last run. This proved to be a fatal mistake.

They ran up and down and round and round, the dogs were starting to lag, they had had a busy night. Finally, the hare managed to find an escape route and took full advantage of it to disappear out of sight. The dogs came back puffing and panting, except one, and that was Pip. It seemed odd. Further investigation revealed him to be very unsteady on his legs, the symptoms progressed until he could no longer even stand up. We tried to coax him along, but it was impossible – he couldn't move. At this stage we both took the situation somewhat lightly and thought he was just tired. But alas, the worst was yet to come. I decided to pick him up and carry him. We were about a mile from home, so would soon be back. On putting him on my shoulders I discovered that he was not only panting, but had developed a twitch in his body. After about fifteen minutes the twitching had become considerably worse, and he seemed to be in quite a lot of pain. It was then that we changed our plans. Jim would go back home and get his van and I would stay with Pip and then take him to a local vet.

It seemed hours before Jim arrived with our transport, I was so pleased to see him return. I grew more and more anxious for the dog as he was now frothing at the mouth and his breathing became more shallow. At this stage I wondered if perhaps he had been poisoned.

We put Pip in the van and made off for the vet. After about a minute travelling, Pip gave out an ear-piercing howl, the pain he was experiencing was obviously too much, after then he went into a coma. By the time we arrived at the vet Pip was all but dead. The vet took the dog in, told us there was nothing we could do, and to please call back in the morning.

We went back home feeling very sick and empty, insisting and assuring ourselves that we were not responsible for what had happened.

But of course, we were responsible for the dog had been severely over-run, a hard lesson we had learned. It is possible that he may have had a weakness of heart or lungs – but very doubtful.

Looking back, it seemed such a shame that a dog like Pip came to such a terrible end.

Some Lamping Hazards

The hazards of lamping are many, one of course I have just mentioned, but there are a lot more things that can go wrong for both lamper and dogs. I was out coursing hares a while ago with a friend, my dogs had a fair few courses and now it was my mate's turn with his dog. We walked a distance before we came to our next hare, and then he was spotted – a good size hare, squatting well out into the centre of the field.

The dog was slipped. He ran directly to the hare and as he approached, the hare heard his advance and broke cover. We stood still and watched as both hare and dog chased up and down the length of the field, until the hare made a quick turn and headed for a barbed wire fence and was underneath as quick as a flash with dog fast on his tail. I guess you can guess what's coming next. The dog was either going so fast or he just didn't see the fence coming that he hit it full on. With an ear-piercing shriek, he came to a stop. We rushed over to see the amount of damage. We found he had ended up the other side of the fence and had carried on with the course. He had no chance of catching the long-gone hare now – but he had a damn good try.

Eventually the dog returned and on putting the lamp on him we could immediately see a lot of blood on both his forelegs. On a closer inspection, he was in quite a bad way. There was a five-inch tear on his neck and a cut on his side. Both legs were badly swollen by now and obviously making his walking very painful indeed. Once again, one of us sat with him whilst the other went for transport. It wasn't long before the dog was home and attended to and another very expensive night for my mate.

There is always a good risk of serious injury on a ploughed field, especially if there is flint about. On one occasion I ran Belle on what seemed to be a good clean field, she had about two good courses on hares, when the last course came to an end and I could pick her shining eyes out with the lamp, but when I called her back, she wouldn't come. After calling for some considerable time with no joy, I walked up to her to find her lying on her side with a foot pad sliced in two, blood gushing everywhere. I quickly bound her foot and made for the nearest vet. After the usual injections and stitches I returned home with a very poorly dog. It seems funny to me that nine times out of ten when any of the dogs get hurt and need a vet's attention – it's always on a Sunday! Sod's Law I suppose.

Another lamping hazard that springs to my mind is 'Brock' or to the layman, the Badger.

Now the Badger is one of the strongest animals a dog is likely to come across when lamping. There really isn't much more one can say about pursuing a badger, except that it is totally illegal to hunt them and the fine if caught, would be extremely high. What's more they can kill or badly maim a good dog. I fail to understand why these animals should be hunted down as the pelts are generally tatty, so not much if any money to be earned on that score – and they are not edible. Which to me means a total waste of time, and the waste of one of our most beautiful wild animals which are becoming harder and harder to see every year.

I think the ultimate danger for both dog and lamper is by far an irate Gamekeeper! There are many Keepers who would take great pleasure in shooting a dog and score a complete victory over what he considers the biggest threat to his job (the Poacher). I know of some Keepers who have openly bragged of having Lurchers hung on a gibbet along with other vermin. Gamekeepers have taken a very hard step to ensure that the land they keep is free from pests and that there is plenty of shooting for good Payers in winter months,

They have become very sophisticated with the right kind of transport, and even work large areas in groups. Sometimes as many as ten all with Walkie Talkies. If anyone finds themselves face to face with a man holding a radio in the middle of the night – BEWARE – he has a friend or two not so far away.

Having said all that, it is impossible for the Keepers to be out looking for Poachers every night, especially in winter. He will find it hard to call on other Keepers to help him on a patrol as they are invariably in the same busy position.

I have heard Lampers discussing putting a bad penny Keeper out of a job, by raiding his pheasant pens and emptying his land of as much game as possible, and believe me it is usually achieved with some good organisation. I haven't written this in hope that a Gamekeeper will one day read it and back off from a Poacher when he sees one But a Keeper must understand that most Poachers think the world of their hunting companions and to have one trapped or shot by a Keeper is really pushing things too far. The Poacher calls all the hosts as he is the only one who knows where, how and when, he is going Poaching. He can wipe out a pen or two of pheasants in just one night.

Generally speaking, Poachers are not greedy people, ok some are 'professional', and they have a living to make, so they take more than most. But small time Poachers are simply out for the freedom of the night, to see their dogs at work and to take a small reward. They are not – (Contrary to popular belief) – out to damage people's property or to be cruel to any animal they see. In fact, most have a very deep and lasting respect for the countryside and its ways.

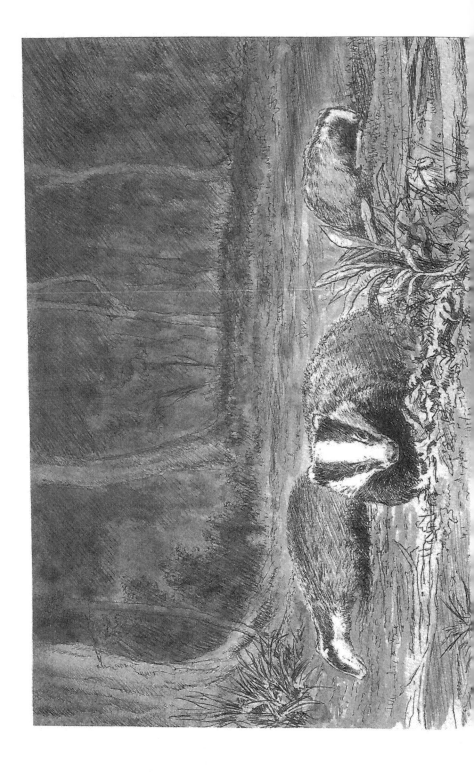

Early Days

A great deal of hunting men are not made, they are born. It just seems to be in them from the time they are born. I have always, as long as I can remember, walked fields, fished rivers and streams for anything I could find. My poor old Mum and Dad at times were nearly out of their minds with worry about what they would find in my bedroom or shed, when I was at home.

I remember one of my early encounters with an animal was one Sunday morning. My two sisters and I attended the local Sunday School and unfortunately the teacher in her wisdom, decided to talk about Jesus – referring to him as the Shepherd of us – His Flock. Now for some strange reason, having just absorbed what I had just heard, my mind began to wander far away across the fields – to sheep. As soon as the lesson of the day had finished, I let my sisters lead the way home while I lingered back until out of sight, and then off to my field of sheep. I remember leaning on the fence just watching. It all became far too much for me, I just had to have one, so into the field I took the smallest one I could see. Looking back, it must have been but a few hours old, as it still had its wet cord attached to it. I was so pleased to get it home safely, only to be seen trying to smuggle it in the back way – by Mum. There was a look of horror on her face, she peered down on me and said.

'Where did that come from?'

Ah. 'I found it.' I replied.

'Rubbish,' came the answer. 'Get the poor little lamb back to its mother and quickly. Its mother will be crying for it.'

I duly returned the lamb to its mother, who was extremely glad to see it!

My own mother must have thought she had brought a small-time rustler into the world, she appeared to have no sense of humour at all over that episode. I also as a youngster enjoyed nothing more than walking upstream watching for the point of entry of a trout into its weedy hideaway. A small amount of mud which the fish had disturbed flowing out of the weed gives his position away. Approaching slowly and quietly as possible, hands into the weed in rhythm with the sway of the weed, pushing slowly through, fingers spread, and then suddenly you feel the slippery flanks of the trout. Carry on up the sides of its body until your fingers are just below the gills, and slowly squeeze. Once you have got a firm grip, hook him out onto the bank where your mate is eagerly waiting to put him in the bag. On a good day we would catch an average of twenty good sized trout. We had literally hours and hours of what we considered to be harmless fun.

Unfortunately, along came the 'trout farm', quite a large number were built around our old fishing grounds. These terrible places that ruin the stream below, bring along with them 'Water Bailiffs', filthy water and trout that taste like cotton wool. For us kids it seemed as if we had had our playing grounds wiped out from underneath us.

As we became older and wiser to the world and its ways, and in need of extra money, we would regularly make night-time raids on such farms. The rewards were extremely good as trout were selling for about 90p/lb at the time.

I only ever got caught once and went to court over the incident. I think the Magistrate must have felt sorry for me with the pitiful story I gave him – he gave me a fine of £35. I estimated that I must have had about £400 worth from that particular fish farm.

Food For The Birds

In 1973 I joined the Army and found myself stationed down in Devon. I enjoyed the Army very much, but soon found myself without animals. With nothing more to think about than bulling boots, cleaning kit and marching here, there and everywhere. It seemed a good idea that whenever I was home on leave, I would find something to take back to the Barracks with me. I started off with a young Kestrel, I had semi-tamed it and intended to fly it to a lure. I had always loved birds of prey with their speed and skill.

On arriving back at camp, the food for the bird was running out fast – I had to get some more! After work the next day I headed into Exeter city to the pet shop where I purchased every mouse they had on the premises. I kept a few back for breeding to continue the line of food for my Kestrel.

The mice very soon started to breed. I had been keeping the bird and mice in a little room that had been set aside for the drying and ironing of clothes. Within about five or six weeks I was soon well over-run with mice. The only other place I could think of to keep them was my personal locker.

Having put about five weeks of my time into this project without being discovered, I pushed my luck on my next return from leave. This time I had brought back two Barn Owls, beautiful little fluffy things of about a few weeks old. I might hasten to add that I didn't take them from the nest, but a local lad passed them on to me, as he couldn't rear them. I now kept all three birds in the laundry room with a proportion of the mice.

Then came the day when my plan went haywire. There was a full Barrack Inspection! A mate of mine flew down the corridor with a box full of mice and fell straight into the arms of

Sergeant Major West, a massive man with a great big pigeon chest, handlebar moustache and a voice that could burst an ear drum at twenty paces! We were caught! All the Officers came to have a look at this created menagerie, they stared in disbelief at the mice running all over the highly polished -floor, and the birds which were sat one, two, and three on the handle of a broom.

I ended up 'on the carpet' so to speak – and the birds and mice ended up in Paignton Zoo, Devon. A message was sent to my parents to ask if they would please 'double check' that I had nothing live on me when I returned to camp in future.

A Few Extra Bob

I had a fairly serous back injury some years ago, which meant that I was off work for nearly a year. In that time, I found myself very short of money. My parents were not too well off and couldn't afford to keep me for next to nothing, which was just about what I was receiving in sick pay.

So, I subsidised it by poaching pheasants, hare, rabbit and fish, on a weekly basis which made my money up to a good weekly wage. I had a very good market for my wares, a local Fish and Game Shop. They were very discreet and good payers, never letting me down on anything I took to them.

I don't think I would like to poach on a permanent basis now, as Gamekeepers and the Police are well set up for dealing with a Poacher, and the fines and penalties are very severe now.

I came very close to being caught in my year on the sick. I was spotted by Gamekeepers on more than one occasion setting snares and walking with a box of ferrets over my shoulder. There were signed statements by both Keepers and witnesses awaiting at the Police Station. All that was needed – was my confession.

What saved my skin on more than one occasion was the fact that I would never admit to doing anything, and I was never caught either selling or carrying anything.

The business side of things was done late evening or about 4.30am, when very few people were about.

I had a very good year, which I shall never forget. It was very hard work and mentally tiring wondering who was watching and where should I go next. But at the same time – good fun.

The Foxes Visit

A farmer gave me a ring this evening and asked me if I would go and see him. Apparently, a fox had been in his chicken house the night before and caused absolute havoc. He had lost all but one of the birds, a grand total of twelve birds had been killed.

Over the past few years I have become quite expert at shooting or snaring foxes, and word is slowly getting around. I charge a small fee for my work and am usually successful.

This particular Fox had given trouble on another nearby farm. So, I started to take a good look around the small paddock in which the chicken house was situated, to see if I would find any trace of the foxes run. I followed the familiar trail of feathers, they twisted and turned across the field until eventually they disappeared into some undergrowth. It was plain to see that the hole that had been made was often used by a fox, well-trodden and hair from the foxes' flanks and brush that had been pulled as he passed through. This was definitely the place to set a snare. The hole was so perfectly round that it was easy to judge the height at which to set the snare.

The snare set – it was all down to waiting. I set the four other snares I had with me in various places and went about my way.

The morning of the tenth, I was up bright and early and straight off to see if I had had any luck in catching Reynard. But nothing. I wold check again later.

As soon as I had finished my days' work, I was off again. It was not very likely that I would have caught a fox in the daytime with a wire. But anything is possible as foxes will sometimes hunt in daytime at this time of year, especially if they are feeding young.

I had taken Belle with me and as I checked round once more to find nothing, I started to wander back to the van. All; of a sudden Belle leapt about two feet off the ground in front of me and gave a yelp I went to investigate as she was limping quite badly. On my looking closely, just above the stopper pad were two little punctures. It occurred to me straight away as to what had happened. It was plainly an Adder bite.

There is no immediate panic when a dog gets bitten unless it is a very small dog. An average size dog can go for a considerable time before it becomes too panful to walk. Nevertheless, as I was not too far from my vets' house, I called in to see him. He soon put Belle right with a quick but expensive jab. She hobbled about for the next fortnight on three legs and seemed to enjoy all the fuss that was being made of her. The following morning, I returned to my snares to find one dead dog fox, it was quite old, with teeth well-worn and coat dull and matted. I untangled him from the wire, presented him to the farmer, collected my fee – 'which nearly paid for Belle's Jab' – then went on my way.

Another satisfied customer I left behind me!

Meg's First Fox

Saturday saw me out on another of my night-time excursions. This time to a very interesting set of fields where game is plentiful on the right night, and this was it. Very dark and good strong breeze to muffle any noises I might make.

I had taken both dogs with me again, it is becoming quite a habit to take both. I know a lot of Lampers who wouldn't dream of running two dogs at the same time for fear of collisions, or – one dog obstructing the other, and indeed, I found that so when I first started. I have also found that when two dogs become used to each other and learn how the other works, it can be quite an advantage I certainly wouldn't say that you get twice as much, but they can aid each other when it comes to lamping a hare, etc.

I had lamped about three of the fields and just approaching the fourth when I gave a quick flash of the beam to reveal a fox halfway across the field. As I was on the right side of the wind I decided to (call the fox up), this is achieved by sucking loudly on the back of one's hand, this making a squeaky noise. The fox, who has not been tricked this way before, will almost certainly advance to the source of the noise in the hope that it will be some injured animal on which he can feast.

Periodically flashing the beam to reveal the fox's approach, I let go of Meg who immediately was hard on our fox. It didn't take too long until she was right behind him, bearing in mind she has never actually had a fox yet. When she left my side this time, she seemed very much keener.

The course seemed to go on for ages. The fox turning this way and that. But Meg stayed right behind refusing to be shaken off. It is really amazing just how fast a fox can turn, they seem to be running full speed one way and as quick as lightening turn on a sixpence without losing any speed.

Just as the fox turned one more time, Meg put on extra speed and in she went, from where I stood I could see the fox upside down. Meg seemed to be well and truly in command of the situation. I was taken aback that Meg at last had actually got a hold on a fox that I ran as fast as I could toward them. Meg must have wondered what the hell I was doing running up to her like that, that she let go of the fox and ran about ten yards away from me. The fox took but a few seconds to recover and promptly made for the nearest hedge. The last I saw of him was his two bright eyes peering through from the other side of a bush.

After inspecting Meg, I made sure she hadn't been bitten or torn in any way, I made my way on. It started to shower with rain as I went, but the night was still young.

Nothing more was to be seen in the last field, owing to our little disturbance, and so to the next. On peering over the field gate, I saw the field was being used for grazing sheep.

I consider that my dogs are completely stock safe, owing to the fact that as soon as my pups have had the necessary injections to be taken out, I take them over to a sheep farmer who allows me to introduce my young dogs to a ram, who will butt them around a few times. If this practise is supervised properly, no real harm can come to a pup. The point being that it has a lifelong effect on the dog and it never seems to want to go near sheep again.

It seems such a pity that some Lurcher men do not take the time in training their dogs to be safe where farm stock are concerned, as it is not helping our cause at all. So many Land Owners and Tenants are very reluctant to let Lampers on their land these days, and I am sure that unsafe dogs are one of the reasons why. In fact, I have been out with a Lamper on one occasion and found ourselves among sheep, asking my mate 'Are your dogs ok with sheep?',

'Sure, they are.' Came the reply.

Only then to slip both dogs on a hare. The dogs ran directly to the sheep and in a few minutes, all hell was let loose with sheep running at top speed into barbed wire, ending up with both dogs tearing lumps out of the sheep, an absolutely disgusting performance of so called (well trained dogs) and the fact of the matter is that no farmer deserves to be confronted with such a mess to his well-tended and cared for stock.

Anyway, to get back to my original nights' lamping. I went through another four fields catching sixteen rabbits and one hare. As always, I have enjoyed my evening immensely, I go home with dogs by my side, very proud of Meg, who has had her first fox. Yes, a very good evening, I think.

Rabbits

Before I go any further, I feel I must write a few notes on some of the wildlife we are blessed with on the 'Isle of Wight'.

To some, what I am about to write will be nothing they didn't already know, but others may not be quite so aware of the animals etc. around us.

I would like to start with the Rabbit. This little dark brown furry creature that seems to be nothing other than an eating and breeding machine, has a very long and interesting history. The Rabbit is not a native of Britain, it was supposedly introduced by the Normans in the Thirteenth Century. This prolific little animal is a natural survivor, which has been more than successful no matter what country it has been introduced to. From the coldest parts of Poland to the hottest parts of Australia it has survived with ease.

The breeding of rabbits is remarkable. They breed throughout the year, but the main season is January to June. The females (Does) give birth to their kittens within twenty-eight days of conception and can re-mate twelve hours after the birth of their young. The average number of young in a litter is five or six. But it can be as many as eight or nine and those young born, can themselves breed within eight to nine weeks. So, as you can imagine, if left alone with nothing to keep the numbers at bay, within a very short time we would be in an awful state, to say the least.

In the early 1900's, as most of us will have read, the rabbit population had exploded. So drastic measures had to be taken and quickly. So, in 1953 we imported something stronger than the rabbit population and far more devastating (to the rabbit, that is). Myxomatosis; this disease wiped out millions of rabbits up and down the country. The first outbreaks of the disease were long before my time, but from what I have seen heard, and read, the sight of these rabbits dead and dying, really were an horrific sight. And as we know this terrible plague is still with us today. Although many rabbits seem to have become somewhat immune to it. Just now and again I come across 'Myxy' and the sight is very unpleasant indeed. Swollen eyelids are the main feature, the swelling is so that it slowly blinds the host. On closer inspection of a rabbit you will see swollen nose, anus and genitals, and the skin becomes very wart-like and the fur very matted so when coming across a myxy rabbit, it is vital that it is put out of its painful misery as soon as possible.

It is now said that the rabbit population is slowly on the increase. I sincerely hope that Myxy is never used in such a way again. After all there are plenty of people around these days who would be only too pleased to rid a farmer of his unwelcome pests.

The rabbit seems to be fair game for a host of predators – cats, weasels, badgers, foxes, certain birds of prey and of course lampers and ferreters. But after all that they still keep breeding and multiplying. I don't imagine they will ever be an endangered species!

Rabbits can literally eat their way from one side of a field to the other, they can devastate a good crop in next to no time. As you go through a field where rabbits have been, it is usual to see places which have been set aside for toiletries – large patches of burnt crop. Rabbits urine contains large amounts of ammonia which does in fact burn and poison large areas of soil. So, you can see the rabbit has had an extremely hard time over the years but is still going strong and there seems to be enough for all.

Rabbits make an excellent meal for any family. The meat is plentiful, lean and reasonably free of fat. Butchers seem to be more interested in buying larger amounts of them than they used to, at around £1.25 per head – one can do quite well for a bit of pocket money!

Hares

The Brown Hare – What an animal! On occasions faster than a greyhound, and can run a hell of a lot further. This remarkable creature, larger than a rabbit, weighing in at an average of five to seven pounds, (I have caught one at eleven pounds, but this was very exceptional) is a much richer brown in colour than a rabbit.

Hares live in wide open spaces, such as arable farm land. They make a shallow scrape in the earth, which is called a Form, and then spend long periods of the day squatting in it. They can be seen breaking the safety of the Form in early evening and venturing out to feed. They graze for most of the night on about any crop that comes to hand, returning to the Form at dawn.

As most will know that camouflage of the hare is brilliant. When I go coursing in winter, it is extremely hard to spot a hare in its Form. My friend's wife actually stood on one whilst out Greyhound Coursing one Saturday afternoon.

Where there is an abundance of hares there are not many rabbits and vice versa. The two just don't mix. Whether or not it has something to do with territory or not, I don't know, but never will there be large numbers of both feeding together.

Hares too are a pretty good breeding machine. They can have three or four litters a year and three to five young per litter. The young (leverets) when born, are fully furred and their eyes are open and stay with mum for about four weeks and then start to wander away. Eventually making a Form of their own, the young themselves can breed within a year. So, it is quite surprising that we don't see as many hares as rabbits.

They have more or less the same number of enemies as the rabbit. I believe that pesticides being sprayed about these days, are responsible for quite a few deaths among the Hare.

Hares that are caught or trapped make a most frightful noise, it is between a shrill and a groan. It is very disturbing to hear and makes one feel very sorry for them. There is no closed season for hunting the hare, but there is a law which forbids the sale of hares between March and July. They don't seem to be very popular with butchers at any other time either, except perhaps in winter months.

Hares can live up to six or eight years, but seldom reach old age as they are hunted by so many. The meat on a hare is very plentiful, but is an acquired taste, not nearly as popular as rabbit. The average pride paid for a good hare these days is around three pounds. Still worth going after.

It is rather disturbing that surveys show that there is a steady fall in the hare population, there is no explanation as to why this should be. It would be such a great shame to see these noble little creatures disappear from our countryside. It is up to us to make sure this does not become a reality.

The Badger

We have all seen him in books and on T.V. What a beautiful animal, with his familiar black and white striped head. He is closely related to the skunk and weasel. The main colour of his body is grey and white on his under belly. The badger is about three feet long when fully grow and stands about one foot high. He consumes a wide variety of food ranging from snails, worms, grubs, lizards, frogs, ice, voles and fruit, to name a few. He has a real weakness for bee's honey, and will break into a hive if he gets the chance. Apparently, the bee can do little if no harm to the badger invading the hive, as badgers have a very thick and touch skin, and any sting would not be able to penetrate.

The badger or brock as was the name given by the Saxons, is an extremely strong animal. He has large forelegs with plenty of muscle, and large front feet which enable him to dig through the hardest ground. Badgers are very sociable animals - and live quite happily in colonies. Their home is called a Set – and is usually situated in a wood. The set isn't usually very well hidden, which is the downfall of many a colony of badgers. They are very clean animals and spend a lot of time grooming themselves. It is said that they change their nesting material very often. Also, they will never foul their nest. They have a set place outside in which to do their business. They sometimes share the set with others. Foxes and rabbits have been known to occupy the same dwelling.

The female, a sow, can have three to four young in a litter, but the mortality rate is high as often only one will survive.

They do much of their foraging for food at night when there is less danger. They are sometimes to be seen during daylight hours, but this is very rare. The best time I have found to watch badgers is just after it has become dark. They are so very interesting to watch, always busy in work and play. They will wander many miles in a night looking for their necessary fill of food and nearly always return home by daylight.

I have already said how strong the badger is and on occasions whilst lamping, I have come across a few badgers and have immediately put my dogs on the lead and walked in the opposite direction. It is a very unwise and cruel man indeed who will allow his dogs to bait the badger, and it can seriously injure or kill one's dogs.

I have already voiced my opinion on pestering brock and all I can say is, that I hope any offender who is caught in pursuit of badger – receives his just rewards.

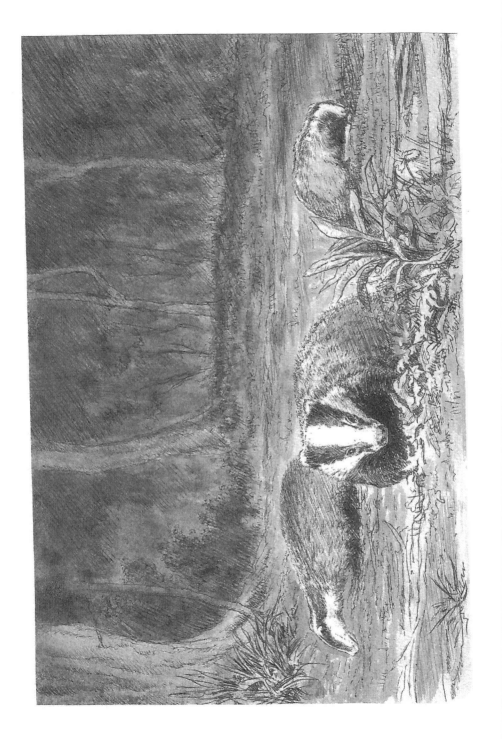

The Red Fox

Again, we all see him at one stage or another, he comes in several colours ranging from black, silver and cross reddish pelt striped with black. In fact, silvers at one time were bred for their pelts, on special farms. But in latter years this practise seems to have died out.

The fox usually makes his home in very thick undergrowth. A very shy animal that goes out of his way to be undetected by man. His diet is again quite wide ranging and consisting of mice, voles, young birds, rabbits, insects and given a chance will take leftovers from a dustbin.

One of the major downfalls of the fox, as we all know, is his habit of raiding poultry houses. He is so cruel and destructive, that when one sees a hunt hard on his tail it is difficult to feel any sympathy with him. On entering a poultry house, he will kill or maim as much as he can, and will only take one bird with him when he leaves, with the rest of the kill he will either leave or half bury them as a larder and return nightly to feast on one or two at a time.

On inspecting a chicken house after a fox has made a visit, it is not unusual to find the heads of the birds ripped off. Any birds that are unfortunate enough to have survived, must be put out of their misery, as they would inure themselves in some way, and if not would probably never lay eggs again. As the shock will have been too much for them. The worst part of all this is that if he is not dealt with, and you restock with chickens, the fox has enough confidence to return – and he will. It is very difficult to make a chicken run fox-proof. I have had birds taken by a fox climbing a six-foot fence to get at them. On that occasion I lost nearly £400 of birds to one fox.

It is true that foxes are very cunning and sly. They are the devil himself to catch. It usually is a case of outwitting him, so as to get your revenge.

The fox is a natural hunter, so it can mean hours of sitting in the cold, wet rain, or snow of winter just waiting for him to turn up. Although the fox is so well hunted, it is still with us good and strong. Surveys show that numbers are on a steady increase. Foxes live in dens or earths, and some earths can go very deep into the ground.

The young cubs of a fox are born in spring and are reared by the vixen alone in most cases. The vixen makes every effort to keep her young away from any danger. If the young wander too far from safety she will pick them up and return them to the earth. If the vixen thinks her earth has been discovered by man, she will simply move home to some where safer. Sometimes taking over a rabbit burrow if it is large enough.

The young will venture away from the earth, getting further and further away until around autumn they will leave altogether. They don't immediately make a den, they will lay in deep undergrowth until a mate has been found. They can fend for themselves quite easily by four months old and are mature at a year old. Foxes have a very acute sense of hearing and smell, it is very unusual to come face to face with one, as he will have detected you coming long before.

On watching foxes from a distance, they are very busy working animals. They scan hedgerows and fields with nose continually on the ground searching for food. They hunt all night long, leaving home at dusk and returning when full. Foxes are known to have a very keen appetite and never seem satisfied on a night's catch.

It is known for people to try and make pets from foxes. It really is a bad idea. Foxes always retain a wild streak and should never be trusted. Although they are beautiful looking animals, one should never try domesticating them. They are much better off in the wild and it really would be cruel to keep them as pets.

There is as we all know a lot of argument as to whether foxes should be hunted now. I can assure you that in my view there is a real need to keep fox numbers at bay. Mainly because of the damage they do to chickens and young pheasant chicks etc. The arguments are very strong for and against hunting, especially with hounds, but ninety percent of the so-called Anti's have never been on the receiving end of a fox's carnage.

Foxes are at the moment a pest and it is totally legal to kill a fox. I fear in the future things may change, and if so, we will be over-run with the fox that does so much damage to our friends.

A Successful Weekend

A trip to the mainland was long overdue, so I promptly booked myself and the van on to the Ferry.

In Winter months the fare for the car and driver isn't too bad, but on this occasion, we were still on summer rate, but I couldn't let this expense hold me back any longer. Having practically come to a standstill through the summer with my hunting, just barely keeping the dogs ticking over (fitness wise), I was quite prepared to pay any amount (within reason) for a night or two's good Lamping, as was to be found on the Mainland.

I usually set off around 6 o'clock on a Friday night the journey is not too long, about one hour in all. Leaving nice and early gives me enough time to visit my family and maybe a pint or two with my nephew, when he is on leave from the Army. He is always keen to escort me on Lamping trips. I enjoy having him along as he is very strong (in the arm) and makes an excellent carry man.

I have some very good legitimate running ground on the Mainland. It is a real treat to go somewhere that isn't Lamped too often and on which of course there is an abundance of game ranging from deer to pheasant. So, Friday night turned out to be a Lampers' Dream. Windy, dark and quite cool.

We started off in some very large rolling fields that I know very well. From walking round the perimeter of one field to the top, one can sweep the whole field with the beam, and detect any quarry that is feeding, and luck was with us. I counted about seven hares in all. So, picking out the nearest and slowly walking towards it, I let both the dogs go. The dogs were very keen to be released from the slips. Sometimes I get a gut feeling when I see the dogs go and can almost predict whether the quarry will be caught or not.

The dogs got nearer and nearer to the still squatting hare, they must have been about fifteen yards from him when he sensed danger and broke cover. The course was very short indeed. Meg was the lead dog, she very soon turned the hare right into Belle's path, and the course was over in a matter of seconds. A good-sized hare brought back to hand. Quickly handing over the hare to my nephew and scanning the field once more, it was not long before I spotted another hare in squat, further down the field. The dogs that were running free followed the beam until they too spotted the hare and were off. Again, it was not too long before the hare was on the run. This time it was neck and neck with the dogs as they went up and down the field, until the hare made the mistake of trying to get through a rather thick hedge and couldn't make it. The dogs were on him in a flash and that was number two hare caught and retrieved.

The night was still very young and we'd had a very good start.

Going on to the adjoining field we see yet another hare. Pushing my luck, I slip the dogs once more. This hare must have been alerted by the noises of the last two, because he was off at a very high speed. The dogs were lagging a bit at this stage as they had not yet got their breath back from the last course., The hare out-turned them several times before finally turning towards us. It is really good to see a hare or rabbit coming straight towards you pursued by a couple of dogs, it would make an excellent photograph if one was quick enough to take one.

The hare passed within about ten feet of us and the dogs were beginning to slow as the course was long and hard. Whenever I used to have a rabbit or hare run towards me like that, the favourite trick was to stick out a foot and trip him up.

The last time I did that I was first hit by the hare who ran straight into my ankle at high speed. (I thought I had broken my ankle) and then was hit by two dogs that were after the hare. I was sent head over heels, landing on my back with my lamping box stuck into my should blades. I got up bruised and battered and feeling a complete ass, and I vowed never to make the same mistake again.

We returned to the van, pleased with our start and drove off to a nearby golf course. In the past I have had some good catches on this land and this night was no exception. As soon as I turned on the lamp there were rabbits running everywhere, I often find that if the rabbits seem a bit uneasy, if you make a slight noise, perhaps crack a small branch or click your fingers, you will find that a lot of the rabbits that were making for cover will immediately squat. It is then possible to pick and choose which to go for.

This particular golf course is very large and takes a fair time to walk round. But it is usually well worth it and it was. We had fifteen rabbits altogether, again not too bad. We returned the catch once more to the van as my nephew was complaining about the weight. Then a nice cup of tea from the flask, after which we returned to the golf course, not for another walk round it, but to get to some fields on the other side. Having walked about three quarters of a mile to reach them, only to find that they hadn't yet been cut, which was a shame because they are quite good at the right time of year.

So, we stood and discussed which land we should do next. On giving he field one last scan with the beam, I spotted four or five sets of eyes peering at us. It didn't take long to discover what they belonged to – Roe Deer. We stood and watched for some time. Bu the odds were against us, with the long corn and the distance the deer were far from us. We agreed to give them a miss this time. So back to the van we went.

Our next port of call, was some ten miles awa
good ground with plenty of rabbits. On our arrival we
outside the farmhouse and had yet another cup of te
work this lamping you know!). Then after our break, on with
the walking. This place is well known for its fox population and
unfortunately there is no local hunt to keep the numbers down.
We spoke on the way that Meg may stand a good chance of
getting a fox here.

We started off along the main track that leads to the
fields, as I have said this is good ground. But the gateways
and fences leave a lot to be desired. I think there are only
about two gates out of the whole lot that open properly. The
others you have to climb over and the fences are so tight it's a
real pain trying to get through, as getting snagged up is almost
inevitable.

We reach the beginning of the fields and put the lamp
on. I saw a couple of rabbits on the far side of the field but
absolutely nothing to be seen elsewhere. So on to the next
field which turned out to be the same as the last. So, on again
to the next That was a bit more like it, there were a few rabbits
sat out in the middle so releasing the dogs from the leads, off
they went. The first rabbit came quickly and was retrieved by
Belle. The second was Meg's and so was the third. We walked
a bit further into the field when I saw a squatter not too far
from the hedge. I quickly put Meg back on the slip lead and
sent Belle on. The reason I chose Belle for this rabbit is,
because she will stalk a rabbit or hare that is sitting tight in a
beam. She was on her way walking slowly down the beam of
light with her wits about her. It is very hard for a dog to see a
squatter unless it saw her move first, or it moves slightly while
in squat. On and on she went stopping now and again for my
direction, 'go on Belle' I said, and on she went. She stopped
again feet from the rabbit, suddenly he broke cover and ran
towards the hedge. Belle was very close behind him. As the
rabbit got nearer and nearer to safety from the hedge, I flicked
my lamp by wavering it rapidly from side to side, thus putting

off a rabbit from finding a hole in a hedge in which to escape. I have prevented many an escape by using this method.

The rabbit was totally confused by my actions and hesitated at the hedge giving Belle a chance to make up lost ground, I saw her strike – and another one for the bag.

As we walked on round the fields there was not so much more catching. But we did see a badger, the first one I have ever seen on this land. He seemed aware that we were watching him. But didn't take too much notice of us apart from putting his nose in the air and having a good sniff in our direction. We decided to call it a night, as we would be out again tomorrow night, and we didn't want to overdo things with the dogs.

Saturday night saw us out at about 7 o'clock. We had left early enough to visit a good-sized area of land that is very well known for the quantity of game that it holds.

We parked the van on the side of a small track which leads down to the wide-open valley of fields. On walking down and keeping well under cover of the hedgerow, we spotted a reasonable size herd of Roe Deer. I hadn't taken my dogs with me at this stage, as this area is under very good surveillance (well keepered), and it would have been foolish to be seen with them. So, we left the safely in the van. We walked for about three miles and saw even more deer, also plenty of hare and rabbits.

We later returned to the small village a few miles down the road, where we discussed our plan of action for later on, over a few pints of beer. A little tip for the poachers amongst you is, if entering a public house before our night's work starts – don't drink too much, because as in war time (walls have ears) in these old country pubs you can bet there is always someone who is only too pleased to listen to someone else's conversation and take great pleasure in passing it on, until eventually the information enters the wrong ear. Which in turn leads to endless trouble and all because beer loosens tongues. (Beware!)

We started our night's lamping by visiting some different fields than the ones we visited earlier, the reason being, that we wanted to be as sure as we could. That no one would be around when we went back to our original fields.

So, the night's lamping began on land that we had permission to be on. I have never caught much on it but at least it's safe. We caught three rabbits on it. There didn't seem to be much at all. The reason could well have been that we saw four foxes over there altogether and when foxes are on the prowl the rabbits just don't come out. So back to the van to wait out our time.

We took a slow drive back to the land that we looked at earlier in the evening. On our arrival we had a quick cup of tea, and a little chat as to which way we should go. Five minutes later we were off. We didn't need to go far before we came across the roe deer, about six of them were laying down well out in the field. We thought the situation out and decided to walk down the right-hand side of the field with the wind in our faces, and undercover of the hedge. It worked a treat! We were able to get quite close to the dozing deer without them detecting us. I flashed the beam of the lamp in their direction. Once more, good. They were still there. We left the hedgerow behind us and walked directly toward the deer. I wanted to get as close as I could to them before releasing the dogs. Belle has taken deer before, but Meg had never even seen one up til now. It will be interesting to see her reaction!

I thought by now I was as close as I was likely to get, without the whole herd disappearing. So the dogs have spotted one that moved slightly. Now is the time, both dogs slipped from their leads and on their way.

As the dogs closed in on the deer there was a bit of confusion as the herd broke up. Belle had obviously picked out the one she was going for Meg had picked hers, and in my mind, I had picked mine. The problem being that none of us seemed to agree. It is very easy in a situation like that to lose your head and flash the beam of your lamp from one to another, the ultimate result being that you go home empty handed. No, it's far better to make up your mind and stick to it. Pick out one with the beam and keep it on it. The dogs will follow your direction with the light. That is exactly what I had to do. The dogs soon appeared back in the beam and were in hot pursuit of the deer. The course lasted about one and a half minutes. The good-sized deer was soon brought down by both dogs held by the throat and was quickly dealt with.

We left this place as soon as we got back to the van. A good successful night we'd had, finishing off a good weekend's lamping I had been yearning for.

Things That Go Bump In The Night

I enjoy my Lamping very much and feel I am almost addicted to it. Some of the things that can happen whiles one is out can be funny, scary and sometimes hair-raising.

I used to poach on one of the large estates on the Isle of Wight. Now considering the amount of time that I spend out nightly, I rarely come across other lampers on my travels. However, this night, I was walking over my estate on my own with just one dog (Belle) when I saw in the distance a strong beam of light, scanning the field directly in front of me. I crouched down and watched for about five minutes. The beam of the unknown lamper found a rabbit, and after a short course I saw an Alsatian-like dog pick up the rabbit. Out went the light and the dog disappeared.

The beam of light flashed on and off as the lamper went on. It reminded me of a lighthouse. He seemed to be quite careless of where the beam shone. By the direction in which he headed, I knew that if I back tracked on myself and took a sharp left turn on to a track, then walked pretty fast, I would be able to head him off and come face to face with the man who was beating me to my night's bag.

This I did, and after about twenty minutes the an was within ten or fifteen yards from me. I could see the silhouette of two large dogs and the man against the skyline. I let him come just a little closer, then stood up and said 'Can I help you?' in a loud voice. By this time the beam of my lamp was pointing directly in his face. The man was so scared he turned and started to run, he tripped over one of his dogs on the way and fell over, landing with a loud thud on the ground. He stayed there motionless until I got up to him. Once again, I put my beam on hm. By this time, he was a quivering nervous wreck, and looking at him just laying there I felt so sorry for him. I had to come clean.

'Sorry Mate, did I give you a scare?' I said.

'Yes, you bloody did, you bastard,' came the reply. 'Who the hell are you?' came the second question.

I told him who I was, and helped him back to his feet. By this time the colour seemed to be coming back to his face. Again, I apologised to him.

'That's ok Mate,' he said. 'But please promise me, don't ever do that again. 'Ere,' he said. 'Want a fag?'

'Yes, thanks a lot,' as I took one his hand was shaking so much, that I had a job to get one out of the packet.

When he had calmed down, we chatted for a while about dogs. The dogs that he had with him were Alsatian x Greyhound. He said they were the best dogs he had ever owned, and both were noted fox killers. When our little chat came to a close, we both went on our separate ways.

'See you again,' I said.

'Not if I see you first,' came the reply.

And I've never seen him from that day to this.

I remember a similar instance that happened to me some years ago. I had purchased Belle as a pup at about four months old. At the time I was the proud owner of a smallholding in Wootton, on the Isle of Wight. Belle was supposed to be a deterrent to any chicken stealing fox that came too close to the birds that ran free range over the land. It was not until a good friend put me right on what the capabilities of a lurcher were. After seeing my mate's dog working day and night, I was so impressed, I realised that there was much more to life than mucking out pigs and collecting chicken eggs. It was about time to train my pup to do the same as my mate's had done.

The training was easy, the dog was bright, and had lots of hunting instincts, which was just as well as I hadn't done anything quite like it before.

The time came when a small battery was purchased, a lamp and a bag to put the catch in. Night after night I went out and didn't catch a thing. When I got home, I would say to my wife – 'this Dog's no good at all, she couldn't catch a cold!'

And then one night, I went out and spotted a squatter; putting Belle on a slip I walked very slowly up to the rabbit. I knew Belle had seen it as she was tugging on the lead. I released her and she lurched forward, striking and catching her very first rabbit. To my surprise she returned it to hand. I was shaking with excitement so much that on taking the rabbit from her mouth, I was so clumsy that it kicked free from my hands and ran straight into a bush.

From that time the seed was set, I could no longer sit around in the evenings. I had to be out. I was lucky to have such a good start, as the land adjoining mine I had complete access over and there was an abundance of rabbits.

Some parts of Wootton are very heavily wooded and in one wood an old tramp lives. His home is a caravan, and lives with about four dogs for company. The old boy enjoys his pint at the local, but nine times out of ten, he tends to overdo things ands then one can find him wandering home over the fields or just sitting in the hedge trying to sober up after pub hours. His dress obviously leaves a lot to be desired. He wears an old black three-quarter length coat, black boots (about three sizes too big for him) with no laces and a black trilby hat with a pheasant feather stuck on the side. I must admit not a pleasant sight in the day, let alone at night. Anyway, on with my story.

At this stage I was out with Belle about three or four times a week. She was catching rabbits now quite regularly. I had already become addicted to the sport.

One very dark but still night, I decided to go and do some lamping. I started off on my own land and then ventured on to my neighbours. I remember the nights were getting very cold, so I wrapped up warm with my collar up, and my hat pulled over my ears. So, my sense of hearing wasn't quite what it should have been. I must have been walking for about an hour and a half and decided to look in just one more field, which involved climbing over a rusty old gate half obstructed by overhanging branches of trees. I made my way halfway over the gate and was just about to put my other leg over when a very cold hand touched mine, which was on the top run of the gate, and a voice said "Ere, cold night in'it.' I felt every hair on my back stand up. I think at one stage I even saw my life flash before my eyes. I screamed out loud, so loud in fact, that it must have scared the dog, as the last I saw of her, she was running for home.

The strange voice had come from old Bill the Tramp, who had decided to take a breather and lean on the gate for support until his legs co-ordinated better with his brain, long enough to get him home.

I can't write down what I said to him that night, as it is still something of a blur! But I can assure you it wasn't very pleasant. I did mention to him that it would be a good idea if he would whistle when he walked at night to let people know where he was. Every time I see old Bill now, day or night, he is always whistling!

One night in 1986 I was out lamping with my dog, on some land on which I had permission. Having walked for about an hour and realised that here wasn't much to be had in those particular fields. I decided to go in search of a better place. After wandering up some disused track roads I ended up at Carisbrooke Castle. Now the Castle has many ghost stories which have been attached to it over the years. I am not all that familiar with most of them. But like most Castles have a history of battles that took place in them, and the bloodshed, gives rise to many a ghost story.

This particular night there was just a very slight breeze, very dark and mild. I had already searched various fields around the Castle area and found nothing. So as a last resort I shone the beam from my lamp in the immediate grounds of the Castle.

I was stood looking at the top of a small valley looking towards the walls of the Castle. I had a very good field of vision, with no obstructions. As the beam scanned the area it was then I spotted a rabbit feeding about halfway up the other side of the valley. Belle my dog was ready, so I sent her on. She ran about forty yards toward the rabbit, stopped dead I her tracks, turned and came straight back. When she arrived back to heel, she appeared to be very uneasy about something. I couldn't understand it. I knew that she had seen the rabbit. I tried to send her on again, but she just would not go. I thought, maybe if I walked a way with her it may have some effect. So off I went. I must have got about some two hundred metres down the side of the valley, when I heard a very strange noise indeed, and can only describe the said noise as resembling a medieval battle taking place. It sounded like a lot of screaming and bawling with the sound of clashing swords and thuds from pieces of wood. I searched the area for the source of the noise, but nothing I didn't go any further toward the Castle, as by this time I was becoming quite worried. On looking behind me there was no sight of Belle whatsoever. So I decided to beat a hasty retreat back to my van.

As I approached, I could see Belle sitting by the back door of the van, she still had that uneasy look about her. I opened the door and she jumped in like a shot and sat as far back inside as she could. I decided it was time to leave and left that place with what can only be described as 'on the hurry up'. With the smell of burning rubber behind me, I have never been back again!

In Search of New Fields

I spend a lot of my free time in daylight hours trying to find new places to go, asking farmers for permission to hunt, and generally mooching around to see what there is to be seen.

In the early summer of last year, I went on such a walk. It was a nice cool morning, the time was about seven-thirty a.m. I walked for what seemed to be mils along discussed footpaths, tracks etc., until I found myself in the middle of nowhere. The footpath I had been walking on, came to an abrupt end and I was now faced with thick rough woodland. My sense of direction is usually pretty good, but on this occasion, I was hopelessly lost.

Trying to retrace my steps proved to be quite impossible, as on the way I had ventured off the beaten track while in search of another, hence I became totally disorientated.

I stood for awhile just trying to think which way to go. After ten minutes or so I had made my mind up to walk straight ahead through the wood in front of me and keep walking until I came upon a road. I struggled over a fence that ran along the outside of the wood, and started beating my way through the thick undergrowth. It was taking much longer than I had expected, to make any progress. Then stopping to take a breather, I could just see what appeared to be, a lot lighter further on. So I walked and as I approached the lightish area of the wood, I could see that it wasn't in fact the end of the wood, but a very large clearing (man-made). It was most strange, the trees had been cut down making a very large circle, there were various objects, such as tree trunks cut into seats, and a large pole in the middle with carvings on it. At first, I thought it was maybe a kiddy's camp. But then, looking on the ground there was a big Pentacle marked out with large flint stone Also there was a trunk of a tree hollowed out on top, with a very large perfectly round stone placed in the hollow on top.

Looking back on the ground I could see it was very well worn. Closer inspection revealed footprints (all going the same way) – round and round. I felt sure this had to be a place that was used for Black Magic practices. (time to go – I think).

I carried on entering the wood once more. I stopped and turned to have one last look, (Creepy) it sent a shudder down my back.

On and on I went eventually finding the end of the wood. A sigh of relief came when I spotted a car going along. I made my way to the road which was instantly recognisable once my feet were finally on the tarmac.

It was a very long slog back to the van. I eventually made it. I don't think I have ever been so glad to see it. In a short time, I was on my way back home. As I pulled into our road there was a great big bang from somewhere underneath the van, I quickly pulled over and lifted the bonnet to find the source of the trouble. This revealed nothing, so back behind the wheel to finish my journey home, only to find that I couldn't put the gear lever into first. It soon became apparent that the loud bang had been my gear box finally giving up. Luckily, I was all but home. About two minutes on foot, so I wasn't entirely stuck, but I do remember thinking 'Oh My God, the Black Magic Worshippers have slapped some sort of curse on me'. I have since heard that there is a very active group of Black Magic Worshippers in that area who are very keen to keep the location of their practices a strict secret. So, Mum's the Word. (Map supplied with S.A.E.!)

A Quick Dash

Eighteen moths ago was the highlight of my entire life, when my wife gave birth to a beautiful baby boy. It was such a joy when the Midwife came out of the hospital theatre and announced 'Mr Martin, you have a very healthy baby boy'. The next eighteen years of my son's life came to me in a flash. I could see it all, the first puppy I would buy him, the first rabbit he would catch with it, and the fun I would have teaching him all I know about hunting.

I am not really sure if it will turn out quite how I would like, but of course, time will tell. He is showing lots of interest in the dogs and will spend long periods of time standing outside their kennel talking gobbledy gook to them. He has also discovered the ferrets in the hutch at the bottom of the garden, and decided to poke a finger through the mesh, just to see what they feel like. One of the ferrets thought he was being given a tit bit and took a bite. Obviously, there were screams that rang out so loud that the entire road must have heard and wondered what the commotion was It ended up with me getting a good telling off from the wife. (all my fault of course). If you know anyone, dear reader, I am now the proud owner of three ferrets, all going free to good homes.

Obviously, having such a young child on our hands, we have been through the inevitable traumas of teething, wind, croup and sickness. But my story begins one night last year when my son had been suffering with a very bad attack of the said wind. My wife Sally, in her wisdom had just given him a small spoonful of Gripe Water, which solved the problem in next to no time I was so amazed at its effect, that I enquired more about it of my Wife, who is a nurse. Because of her profession she tends to go into every detail if a medical question is asked, and I have to say on occasion this an become a bit boring. So, having asked a few questions, I wasn't paying too much attention to what was being said, but I do remember her saying that if ever she was working at night and I was babysitting, the bottle of Gripe Water would be in the cupboard above the sink in the kitchen.

Just before I went to bed that night, I took a last look outside. The wind was really getting up, and it was very dark. In fact, I thought it was too good to miss, so I planned on having a couple of hours sleep and getting up about 2am to do some lamping. This I did. But when I got out of bed, I had the most griping pain in my chest. I thought for one horrible moment that maybe it was a heart attack. It was so painful.

I got myself a cup of tea, sat down and waited to see if the pain would ease. Which in fact it did, after about ten minutes or so. Then it dawned on me it must be indigestion – I thought – (Gripe Water). So, making my way to the cupboard above the sink in the kitchen, as I remembered my wife saying, and still half asleep, reaching into the cupboard and taking out a bottle of clear liquid. 'Ah, this is it', I said to myself. But how much to take? Well if my son had a small spoonful at his size, then I would need two big ones at my size. Grabbing hold of the biggest spoon I could find and filling it up to the brim, I tilted my head back and swallowed. 'Urrk'!

It was horrible, no wonder my son cried when he was being given his. Oh well, and going through the procedure once more – it was still horrible. Never mind, I washed it down with my tea. The pain in my chest was really starting to ease now.

So, clobber on, I got the dogs from their kennel and on my way. I didn't have to go too far before finding some good fields. Shining the beam of my lamp into the first field, I could see seven or eight rabbits. Some of them immediately squatted down as the beam spotted them. I could feel the dogs on the end of their leads trembling with anticipation, so I released them. Put the beam on one of the squatting rabbits and walked slowly toward it. I was about eighteen feet from it, when I got the most terrible feeling. I had to go to the loo –

and quick. Putting out the light and moving quickly to the nearest hedge and relieving myself, the feeling was that I had only just made it. After a few minutes I was back on the hunt. Dogs at the ready and desperate to catch the first rabbit of the night.

Again, I found a rabbit in squat, and once again the same effect on my stomach too place. So, in rapid short sharp jerky movements, I made my way to another hedge.

This process went on about five times, in fact, it absolutely ruined the night. The dogs were plainly fed up and couldn't understand why, just when they had seen a rabbit, the light was put out, making it near impossible for them to catch it.

I returned home as it seemed pointless going on. I finally got to bed about 4.30am and finished off my nights' sleep.

In the morning when I woke my wife enquired how I got on. I explained to her that I didn't get a thing ad told her why.

On reaching into the cupboard she pulled out two bottles containing a clear liquid.

'Which one did you take?' she asked, looking at the half empty bottle I her left hand,

I replied, 'That one.'

She burst into what can only be described as hysterical laughter, and announced that what I had taken was in fact Liquid Paraffin, that we had bought some weeks earlier for one of the dogs with constipation.

Needless to say, I was very embarrassed by the whole situation and have never really lived it down. But I can tell you if ever I wake up with indigestion again, I won't take anything for it. I'll just go back to bed!

Hard Walking

Saturday 8th of October was the first meet of the I.O.W. Coursing Club in 1988.

We have all been looking forward to starting for some time, but the ground of late has been so hard and dry that it would have been irresponsible to run dogs on such hard land.

There was a very good turn out of people and dogs, about seventeen people with around eighteen dogs. The weather was terrible, with a very strong wind, very hard rain and the newly sown fields that were waterlogged made the walking very hard indeed.

It is an odd fact that most people who work with their dogs seem to think that they are really fit, until they enter a ploughed field after a good downfall of rain. That's when they soon change their minds.

As it was the first coursing meet, we all started off at a very brisk pace, the wind behind us and downhill, this all made for easy walking. Everybody chatting and joking, with a mixture of the odd story of hunting on the way.

On reaching the end of the field, and sweeping around to face the opposite direction, the wind and rain now in our faces, the walk now uphill with heavy clinging mud on our boots, the conversation comes to an abrupt end. Faces begin to look pained and everybody begins to look totally fed up – mine included.

It is at times like that, that my mind takes on a new wave, I find myself thinking – 'What a bloody waste of time' or 'I could have stayed at work' or even better 'I could have stayed at home in the warm'. But somehow, we all keep going, the odd one or two seem to disappear out of sight and some just stand on the side of the field and watch. But the majority keep on.

This Saturday, we walked up and down several large fields putting up no hares at all, the excuses were starting to be voiced as to not walking any further, i.e. the weather, bad back, unfit dogs and twisted ankle – which is most popular.

We then finished the section of fields we had been on, and crossed over a lane to some new ground. Again, most of the fields were newly sown. We had walked about halfway down the first field, when a large hare broke cover, the first two dogs in the slip (Greyhounds) were released. The course was exactly one minute. The hare was turned a few times before finding its way through a gate and disappearing out of sight.

The effect of the hare getting up was incredible. Conversation started once again, all sicknesses disappeared and people stood on the edge of the fields once again, round the line of walkers. But alas, we walked for about another hour, to find nothing. The hares, we decided, must have been under cover of the hedges, because of the appalling weather. Hopefully the next time we go we'll see some decent coursing.

I don't go coursing every Saturday, as I like to go lamping (my first love) with my dogs at weekends This usually means that if I am out on a Friday night or I want to go out on a Saturday night the dogs are unfit for Saturday afternoon coursing. Or I want to save them for Saturday night. But I try to go as much as I can, it makes for a very pleasant afternoon really, with usually plenty of good conversation about dogs.

The Right Food For The Right Work

Now the very best time of the year is well and truly with us, hunting season. The local Coursing Club is just about to start its Saturday afternoon rambles in search of the hare. The I.O.W. fox hounds are now well into their stride, and I can get in so many more hours of lamping being that the nights are closing in. My dogs are now at their fittest and every lamping session is producing a very good bag.

Each summer that passes seems to be longer than the last, so this is really the best time of the year for me and my fellow lampers.

I started working my dogs regularly in order to get them fit about ten weeks ago, and I have found that it had really paid off so I can now go out with them nearly all night long and I now I won't have to cut the evening short with a tired dog.

This time of year, I am out at least four times a week, so if not manged properly, dogs will lose their condition very fast. Up until a few months ago I was feeding minced tripe (which is becoming quite expensive) with a good helping of cereal meal, to them. I have never been altogether happy with that particular diet, as after a nights' work the dogs would come back looking thin and bedraggled, and then it would take a couple of days good feeding to get them back in shape.

I happened to see a greyhound trainer showing the TV cameras around his premises, on a recent TV Documentary, and low and behold, there was my answer to well fed dogs staring at me from the set. A commercial meat mincer, what magical pieces of equipment these things are.

It took quite a long time to acquire one as they are few and far between, any that do come up for sale are quickly snatched up unless one can move fast enough in the morning to make the first phone call. And to buy a brand new one is out of the question as they range from eight hundred to one thousand pounds.

Mine was advertised in the local paper, and was quickly purchased by yours truly, for the princely sum of One Hundred and Twenty Pounds; it came complete with various fittings and a handful of butcher's knives. Since buying it I have saved a fortune in dog food, as I am given all the leftovers from a local restaurant, plus rabbits, hares and pigeons, and the occasional chicken, are all minced together, making a very palatable diet for my dogs.

I have noticed such a difference with their condition and because the food is free, I am feeding Ad Lib. However, I fear I have bragged too much already, as my lamping mates say that' if it doesn't move fast enough, he'll put it through the mincer'. I have already been offered two light-hearted contracts for getting rid of nagging wives, at least I suppose they were light-hearted?

Looking on the serious side of things, it is possible to give my dogs a much more varied meal, with the right balance of vitamins and of course calcium, from all the bone and now I am more than satisfied – and I know the dogs are too.

The Poacher

There has always been a lot of animosity of course, between the landowners and their gamekeepers, and the poachers.

There are very strong arguments on both sides of the fence, Landowners are after making money from the land, which of course is their right, and the game and the stock on it belongs to them. The poacher takes the view that the landowner is merely a keeper of the land and game which lives on it, and he is entitled to his share.

Landowners tend to cut down trees, uproot hedges and flatten the banks, ending up with a flat landscape and massive fields in order to sow larger crops, and hence, make more money and quicker. So, it is not surprising that the majority of poacher's love and respect the countryside and like to watch all the wildlife. I tend to get uptight at the desecration by the landowners. Obviously, there is a lot more to it. Jealousy to name but one.

The act of poaching has been going on since civilisation started, it was a method of feeding the families of the poor man who had no job or a very low wage. It would have been almost impossible for him and his family to survive unless there was a reasonable supply of decent meat coming into the homes. The penalty if caught for poaching, was very severe in the eighteenth and nineteenth centuries. There were man traps placed in various woods, which could literally snap a man's' leg in two. They were very like a massive gin trap, the penalty for getting caught in one of these, was never ever to walk again in most cases.

Other punishments were deportation, and even worse, death itself. But still poaching was rife, which goes to show just how hard times must have been in those days.

The Gamekeeper has a very hard job. Starting in summer, he is busy with young birds coming up for the season. He is out early in the morning till late at night, keeping an eye on his stock and controlling the vermin, as of curse, the fox is a major predator of young pheasants. A bit later in the year, the young pheasants are put into release pens to harden up before they are let free to roam the ground, just before the shooting season. This is of course, when a keeper must be on his toes. It is very easy for poachers to find the pens and help themselves to the birds. The keeper watches his pens very closely and takes note of any strangers wandering around or any unusual cars that may be parked.

The cost of a single pheasant is very high, it works out at about ten pounds a head, by the time it is shot. So, it is easy to see why a keeper puts so much work into protecting his stock. If any great numbers of his birds disappear in his absence, he is most definitely on the carpet, so to speak.

The poachers are general on the prowl in early Autumn, just after harvest. Getting themselves ready for the season and sighting out new areas and inspecting old. Finding out where the birds are roosting, watching for where the partridge cuvvys are.

The shooting season is without a doubt the busiest time of the year for the keeper. Walking around and watching his stock day and night. Preparing his shoot drives and getting everything ready for the guns, who really pay his wages, so everything has got to work and be exactly right.

It is man's natural instinct to hunt. Everyone of us is born with the ability, but in most its dormant. I don't think it's wrong to hunt as long as cruelty isn't involved. But I know that unfortunately it is on many occasions. Those who do not agree with hunting under any conditions, are of course entitled to their opinion, but I suggest there is an element of ignorance from many anti field sport supporters. A lot consist of

Townspeople, who have never lived in the country, and who know very little of country ways.

One final word on poaching, as it is believed in some circles that there is a lot of money to be made. I can assure you there isn't. Nobody has ever got rich from poaching. Now and again one gets lucky and earns a few extra pounds, but many times you come home with an empty bag and nothing…

The risks a poacher takes these days are obviously not so severe as they used to be, but by all accounts, the penalties are quite bad, with very heavy fines, or even worse – Imprisonment, which of course takes away the very thing that is so dear to a poacher's heart – FREEDOM.

There are a lot of people who like to think of themselves as poachers – or experienced lurcher men. But what many do not realise is poachers and hunters are not made, they are born. I personally have been out with some of these experts and I found them noisy, careless and very unprofessional people, that plainly don't have a clue as to what they were doing.

Good and clever poachers and lampers are like keepers, rarely seen, they keep a very low profile and never brag about how clever they are and keep themselves to themselves.

A Big Surprise

One of my favourite pastimes a few years ago, was to catch the freshwater cray fish. They are about three inches to six inches in length and resemble the lobster very much. They tend to live in fast flowing streams and burrow out holes into the stream banks to live in. The holes, if occupied by a large cray fish, can be as deep as three feet.

The cray fish has a hard-outer skeleton which it sheds to enable the fish to grow larger. It has two claws like that of the lobster, which can give a really painful nip. They live on plant and animal debris, plus insects, worms, small fish and snails.

In the last ten years or so, the cray fish numbers have declined, whether it is because of overfishing or pollution, doesn't seem to be clear. But there is a marked absence of them now in streams where they were once plentiful.

At the time I started fishing for them they were in great demand from the catering trade, so much in fact, that one couldn't catch enough to keep them happy. I would start early in the morning to get myself a good start.

The water was so cold in this stream, that it was sensible to wear the bottom half of a wet suit, which did keep me quite warm, with the long periods of time I was in the water. Plus, they offered some protection against overhanging thorn bushes and sharp edges of reeds.

Usually I took along a friend and his job would be to stand on the bank and follow me as I worked my way upstream. There are several ways of catching the cray fish, one of them is to make, as you would for a lobster, a pot, baited with some rotten meat and left for an hour or two, then return to take your catch. The more pots you put down the bigger the bag. But I have found this method very slow and very time consuming.

Another method is the one I always use. That is to stick your whole arm into the burrow which the cray fish has made. Then push forward until you can feel him sitting right at the end. Sometimes if you are lucky, with a friend or two. The only problem being that he sits with his two claws forward so unless you are very quick in turning him round, he will pinch your fingers with his very sharp claws, and by the end of the day, your fingers will be cut and bleeding with the endless nips you have received, plus the very cold water.

On a god day I would walk about two miles upstream, searching every hole until I was exhausted. On a couple of occasions my arm entered a larger hole than usual, my fingers searching as they travelled to the end, when suddenly I felt something large run over my hand and scurry up my arm from the entrance of the burrow. A great big water rat, came leaping out screaming as he went. I might add at this point, he wasn't the only one doing the screaming! It is such a shock when your mind is tuned in to small hard backed creatures and your fingers find something completely different. About six times the size and furry – with teeth. I could have entered the next Olympics for the world's high jump record, followed closely by the long jump. After such an experience it is hard to get back in the water and carry on. I did go on – but picking and choosing carefully, the holes I would explore.

At the time we were catching cray fish, they were being bought for about three pound and fifty pence, per pound (weight), which was very good indeed. On a good day, we could catch two hundred to two hundred and fifty, and as there is abut eight to a pound (weight), you can see it was very profitable for a day's work.

The stream also held quite a lot of interesting things, such as duck, trout, eels and pike. So, having finished catching cray fish, there was still plenty to occupy our minds.

All this led to a good days hunting and with a good bit of pocket money earned we were more than happy.

Maniac At Large

One night whilst out lamping, I was quietly walking over some of the local fields with my dogs, Meg and Belle. As I approached the end of one field, I had to cross over a small public footpath and into another field. When I heard the loud screams of a young lady, I turned quickly around and flashed my beam down the path in the direction of the scream. I could see some people in the far distance so I kept my lamp on to make sure there was nothing untoward taking place.

Another shout went up. This time a male voice. 'Who's got that bloody light on?' said the voice. I made no attempt to answer and kept the light firmly on the people now getting closer. As I got nearer and nearer, I could make out there were three young girls and two young men. As my lamp was still on, the same question came –

'I said, who's got that bloody light on?'

I still made no answer.

My actions must have really upset the lad, who seemed to be doing all the shouting. As it was just then he started running toward me shouting obscenities. In his hand I could see something shining and then I went cold. The lad was wielding a knife. I was terrified to say the least. I wasn't quite sure whether to turn and run, or stand my ground. I decided on the latter. He got nearer and nearer and just as he came into striking distance, I gave an almighty blow to his face. The knife landed at my feet and the lad fell against the hedge. So I quickly picked up the knife and threw it as far as I could into a field. I then picked up the lad who was quite stunned. He then proceeded to read me the rights of law, told me I had committed an A.B.H. (Actual Bodily Harm), by hitting him, and also theft of his knife. To which I replied –

'Then you must do something about it'

After a very short conversation I then realised that he and his friends were in fact drunk. I suggested that they went quietly on their way – or accompany me to the Police Station. They decided to take my advice and went on their way.

On making enquiries later, I found that the knife man was a local lout, who was always in trouble and well known to the Police. I never had any more trouble with him. But I did hear that he was making veiled threats in my direction. The lad plainly had a lot of growing up to do. I hope he doesn't get too hurt on the way. I must admit that the incident put me on edge for some time after and it doesn't give one a great deal of faith in Human Nature.

Pup's First Catch

For the last six months I have been putting in as much time with my new pup, as has been available. She, as I have maintained before, was one that I kept back for myself from Belle's litter.

I tried when picking from the litter to get one as close to one in nature, colour and size as possible. It was a hell of a job trying to pick the right one. I would spend an hour or so watching the young pups play, finding out the dominant ones, the weak and the shy. The one I picked fitted the bill. It would always be first out of the kennel when the pups were called. Always be first at the food bowl, and appeared to be very bright and interested in the things around it. My choice had been made.

Before any training could begin, I had to wait until all the pups had been sold, as it would have caused too much distraction for my pup. Whilst waiting for the last of the litter to be collected, I would get my pup out of the kennel and play with her on the lawn. I have an old rabbit skin lure which I would tease her with as it is a good idea to get a pup chasing something as soon as possible.

I went very easy on the pup, (which I had named Bonny) and for the first three or more months I never attempted to push her too far with any trick or games for that matter. I think that if one drives a young pup too hard – too soon – the pup is not mentally capable of taking it all in and cannot concentrate for any long periods. The ultimate result being frustration for both the pup and you and a marked reluctance by the pup to want to be in your company. So slow and easy does it with a young pup.

Slightly more serious training came at nearly five months old, it consisted of 'Sit, Stay, Down, and Fetch'. Bonny has been trained in that order. The same way as my other dogs. I have always been successful with my method of training, apart from once, when like an idiot I purchased a dog from an advert in a well-known magazine, without seeing or knowing anything of either parents, and knowing very little of the vendor. The end result being that I was well and truly caught. I ended up with a dog that looked and acted like a ninety-nine percent greyhound, and no matter how I tried the dog seemed to be incapable of learning anything. It was my own fault for ending up with such a dog. But a mistake which I shall never make again. She was eventually given to a very good home, and is still a much-loved pet. While I am on the subject, I often wonder what happens to such dogs, there must be thousands of them born each year and they don't all find good homes. A hell of a lot must end up at the vets to be destroyed, or worse still some owners probably just turn them loose to roam, or even shoot them. It is such a shame that so many dogs end up in this way. But one can go even further with the problem as not every bitch's litter can be a winner. But in the lurcher world, there can be a very casual attitude to the breeding of such dogs. A lot of people just seem to get a dog and a bitch and put them together and produce a litter without thinking of the consequences or potential of the said pups. I think if someone is thinking of breeding Lurchers, it would surely be to their advantage to pick the right type of mate for their dog, and try very hard to better the strain, instead of just another litter of Lurchers; or maybe these dogs are bred by man who can see pound note signs in front of his eyes. So, he doesn't really care what the pups turn out like. A little tip to the lurcher entrepreneur, is it you consider breeding a litter of pups, just for the money, forget it. There is little if any money to be earned. For those who still want to breed, shop around, and find a good mate for your dog and better the performance of your lurcher if possible.

My dog Belle is very bright and her hunting instinct is tremendous, but I have always felt that she wasn't as fast as I would like, (not to be confused with nippy) and she can turn nearly as fast as a rabbit, and has always had good results with hunting. So, the idea when breeding from her was to find a small but very fast dog. This we found.

The dog was a Whippet cross Greyhound. Not a very bright dog, but very fast indeed. He stood twenty-four inches at the shoulder and was a fine-looking dog. By crossing the two, we were looking for a bright dog, with a blue broken coat – about twenty-two inches to twenty-three inches high, plenty of hunting instinct, and one that would be very fast. The Gods' were with us and Belle gave birth to ten pups in all. Six bitches and four dogs. Most were black, which later turned to blue, one was a very light fawn colour, and two were black and white.

A good friend of mine had second pick of the litter. I naturally had first and we were both very pleased with the result. My pup was very easily trained, it didn't take long to teach her the basics. But I just couldn't get her to get the hang of retrieving, no matter how hard I tried. I found myself becoming obsessed with trying to get her to do this seemingly easy task – with no luck. I decided to leave it altogether and try again in a couple of months. In the meantime, I took her to some nearby fields at night to get used to being out late and to teach her as much as possible about the lamp. I walked for a short while with the pup at my side on a slip lead. The night was really dark, with a good breeze blowing, and on shining the beam around, I could see plenty of rabbits feeding well out in the field. I decided to find a squatter and let her have a short run.

In a few minutes I had found my rabbit, he was a bit close to the hedge, but if I could get the right side of him, the pup may stand a chance. I quickly calculated which way to approach and walked very slowly keeping the pup on the lead. I just held her by the collar very slowly walking on until I was standing right by the rabbit. All that remained was to get the pup to see the rabbit, which was still tight in squat. It is quite hard to get an unaware dog to look at something it doesn't even know is there, trying to hold a lamp and pointing a dog's nose in he right direction – is no easy task.

Eventually the rabbit could stand no more and made a break for cover. I quickly let go of the pup, she had of course, chased a couple of rabbits before in daylight when I had been out hedging, but never in these conditions at night. She was soon after the rabbit and as the rabbit approached the hedge, I flicked the lamp to confuse it. This had the desired effect as the rabbit turned instead of going straight into the hedge, which gave the pup valuable time to make up lost ground. I heard her teeth make a loud snap as she turned the rabbit and tried to strike. The rabbit made a panic decision and ran back out into the open field the pup got closer and closer until finally striking and catcher her very first rabbit. To my amazement she brought the rabbit immediately to me, so all my worrying over retrieving was a waste of time. I guess that when they actually have a live rabbit in their mouth, the only place they can think of is to return it to their master.

I have taken her out since and she has caught two more rabbits and each time she is very pleased with herself. She retrieves them with head held high and tail wagging. At the moment I am not taking her out regularly as she still has some growing to do. Plus, her bones are still soft, it doesn't do to do too much too soon.

I am very pleased to hear that most of her litter brothers and sisters are doing just as well. It is a good feeling to hear that what I have tried to do with the breeding of these pups has now at least, come out right.

An Instant Cure

When I purchased my dog Meg, she was about eight weeks old. I was so pleased to purchase a pup from this litter, as they were in popular demand, and being sold on a first come, first served basis. So, it was pull out all the stops and get to the vendor's house as soon as possible. I walked away with my new puppy a very happy man.

I got home in daylight hours, placed her on the lawn in the garden and introduced her to her now home, then took a series of photographs of her for the album

As the evening went on and she began to grow more and more tired, I gently introduced her to her new sleeping quarters, and for good measure, I put Belle in with her for company. The timing was perfect as Belle had just gone through her second season and was obviously feeling quite maternal towards her new friend. Belle immediately snuggled straight up to Meg and made a big fuss of cleaning her, and I witnessed on one occasion, the pup actually sucking from Belle. I was completely astonished at the bond that came so quickly.

It soon became dark and I had stood and watched for long enough. It was time to go in. I switched off the light in the kennel and shut the door behand me.

Sitting indoors that evening I was discussing with my wife, what a good purchase I had made and convincing myself that this was the dog that would beat all dogs in brain, power, speed and sheer style.

I know the dog must be asleep by now I thought, but I must just have one more look. So, I had a quick peep just before going to bed.

As I was getting into bed and pulling on the covers, I thought I heard the Pup give a whine. So, I lay very still for about ten minutes just listening – nothing – 'Oh well I must have imagined it.'

Some time later, just before I fell asleep, you know what it's like, not awake – not asleep, just in limbo. There it was again. I felt sure it was the pup that time. I pulled my senses together and laid quietly listening again. Yes, it was the pup, and the poor thing probably was frightened. I gave my wife, who had been fast asleep – a shake.

'The Puppy's crying,' I said. Do you mind if I bring her in, she must be scared stiff out there in a strange place with a strange dog.

'O.k.' came the reply. 'But only for tonight, and only in the kitchen.'

I was down the stairs in a flash, outside and back with the Pup safely in my arms. I got an old blanket and formed it into a nice puffed up nest shape, placed the pup in the middle, then sat and watched until it once again fell asleep. Just as an afterthought I put a shallow bowl of milk by its side, and for the second time that night – made my way up to my own bed.

I was up bright and early the next morning and straight down to see what damage had been done. I opened the kitchen door – brilliant, nothing, well hardly, just a small puddle in the middle of the tiled floor. No problem. I cleaned it up before the wife came down and she wouldn't know any different. Anyway, it would just go to prove what a clever chap I am picking such a perfect Puppy.

The next few nights were pretty much the same, with a little bit of whining from the pup and me twisting the wife's arm to let me bring her indoors. However, I must admit, the mess in the kitchen was getting worse each time, until finally I had to give in. She had to learn to stay outside at night, and myself learning that I had just made my first fatal mistake, because the next night we made the decision, that if the pup howled, we would just let it carry on until it ran out of steam. It was a hard step to take on a poor little thing like this. But it had to be done.

That night was as predicted. It howled and howled. We both found it very hard to just lay there and do nothing. But as we had decided amongst ourselves and the neighbours, it would only be for a couple of nights.

As soon as possible during daylight hours, I approached our neighbours and apologised for any inconvenience caused. They were all very understanding about it which gave one a good feeling and made one want to boast to the world what a good lot our neighbours were.

We then approached the second night and the third and fourth, and the howling went on and on. I carried on apologising and trying to explain. Our neighbours were now changing slightly – to coin a finer phrase. I was coming up against tired ones, frustrated ones, worn out ones and plain angry ones. Some of them wouldn't even talk to me and some would slam the door in my face – what could I do?

My wife and I put our heads together to try to solve the problem, there were several options open. One of them was that we took the puppy down to the smallholding that we used to own and with the kind permission of the new owner, leave her there in a kennel and let her howl herself out. Thus, learning that nobody would take any notice and hopefully she would stop the terrible noise.

This we did. Now the smallholding was exactly one mile from my home, and although there were houses nearer to it, I didn't think that anyone would be affected by the noise that she may make. I placed her in a nice warm kennel and left quickly. As I drove down the track, I could already hear her starting to whine and I thought to myself 'Be strong willed and just leave her' as I drove on. In a few minutes I was back home, not feeling any better for my actions. I went to open the back door and what was that? I could actually hear the pup howling her head off, or was I imagining it. I stood and listened – Yes it was her. I couldn't believe it. I knew if I didn't get back there quickly someone would call the R.S.P.C.A. I had visions of me ending up in court for cruelty to a dog and being banned from keeping them for life.

I drove at breakneck speed back to the smallholding, I grabbed hold of the pup, not too gently I might add, and took her back home. With one idea gone clean out of the window. I then sad down to think up another.

My second idea turned out to be just as bad as the last. In the morning I rang a local Vet. The telephone conversation went something like this –

Vet – 'Good morning – Mr Vickers Veterinary Surgery'

Me - 'Ah – Good Morning – I wonder, could I speak to a vet please?'

Vet – 'Certainly. Can you tell me the problem?'

Me - 'Yes, I have a young Lurcher pup that is really becoming a problem. I

can't stop her barking at night.

Vet – 'Well, what would you like me to do for you?'

Me - 'Well, I wonder could you debark her for me?'

Vet – 'No, I can't. What an awful thing to suggest. How dare you ring up here

and suggest such a thing. You ought to be reported.'

With that the phone went dead. Back to the drawing board.

For the next week or two, she stayed indoors all snug and warm in the kitchen. I got up every morning and the first chore of the day, would be to clean the kitchen floor, not the best job to have first thing in the morning.

I was now going to work a nervous quivering wreck, every time I shut my eyes, I could hear dogs howling. I felt sure I was heading for a breakdown.

One option which was open to me was to sell or give the dog away. So one evening I put her in the van and made my way over to a friend, who had at the time a lot of dogs of various breeds, in hope that he may have room for one more.

You've guessed it. No – came the answer, he really hadn't enough room for the ones he already had.

The last thing I could think of was to try and find out what other people had done in a similar situation. The next evening, I rang round a few friends. The first suggestion was to acquire a remote-control collar. Apparently, these collars are 'the business', every time the dog makes a noise it simply gives it a mild shock, by pressing a button on the remote-control box, and very soon the dog learns that if it makes a noise of any sort it receives a shock, and thereby keeps quiet. Good idea eh! Apart from the fact that they are very hard to get hold of, <u>and</u> they are totally illegal! The penalties for using one, if caught, are very severe, and when you think about it, they are downright cruel.

Number two suggestion came from a man who has had lurchers for a very long time and indeed, he was the man who first introduced me to the sport. He is well known throughout the Island for his ready wit and good sense of humour, which is good in some respects. But fatal in others as it is very difficult to get a straightforward answer to any question asked. His suggestion was that I should acquire two tin dustbin lids and a large white blanket. Now what one is supposed to do, is hide away in the garden somewhere out of view of the dog, drape the white blanket over your head and wait for the dog to start howling. When she is in full song, run toward her at high speed shouting and at the same time clapping the dustbin lids together as if they were symbols, thus scaring the dog. I am assured she will never make another noise as long as she lives. Good idea I thought – But I just couldn't see myself doing it, for fear of two men in white coats coming to collect me after a tip off from the neighbours!

The final suggestion came from the man that I had purchased the pup from. I gave him a phone call during the evening and explained the situation to him. He laughed at my predicament and told me the very easy cure to the problem.

The solution was simply water. He went on and explained, by losing one's temper with such a dog, or screaming and shouting at it, would do no good at all. Even a good hard slap on the backside has little effect, as it might hurt the dog for but a few minutes, and the pain would soon be gone and forgotten.

The water treatment is the answer. The way it works is so easy, but the timing must be right. What one has to do, is get a good size bucket of water, place yourself outside the dog's kennel and play the waiting game again. When after a while your pup starts its howling again, try and score a direct hit with the cold water. It really is a shock to the dog, it is the last thing they expect to happen. It really has much more effect than a slap, as the cold water will last a long time and the dog will find it hard to forget that experience.

I put the phone down and armed myself with my bucket of water. As I walked down the garden path, she was already howling I shouted at her sternly, something she was quite used to by now, so she ran back inside the kennel. I hid myself away and waited and waited and waited. For one minute I had a horrible thought that maybe she knew I was just outside and wouldn't start barking for fear of being shouted at.

I was just about to leave when I heard her whimper. The whimper progressed to a whine and the whine to a full-blown howl. She was now standing just outside the kennel entrance. Now was my chance. I shot the water in her direction – Whoosh – spot on, I got her full in the face with the very cold water. She was so shocked, she turned to run inside, but misjudged the opening and banged her head on the kennel wall, which thinking about it must have added to the fright. She finally found her way back in and never ventured out again that night.

After that experience she only once tried the howling again, it was a fortnight later. The same treatment was issued and from that time to this, she has always known not to howl. The only problem is, and it's quite mild in comparison to the last, that she hates water, she never walks through puddles, or wants to go swimming. But who cares, you don't find rabbits or hares in puddles or ponds – Do You?

A Bad Night – Turned Good

One Friday night, not so long back, my nephew who had just been granted a weeks' leave from the Army, opened the door and walked in. My wife and I were very pleased to see him, as it had been a long time since his last visit.

After sitting him down with a cup of tea and something to eat, we sat and listened to the stories of his past few months of Army training. Having told us all his news, he asked the fatal question, 'How are the dogs?' and 'Have you been to the mainland lately?' to the first question I answered, 'Fine', and to the latter 'No' but I am thinking of going'.

His face dropped like a stone as he knew what the next line would be. 'Do you fancy coming with me?' I asked, and before he could answer, I said, 'Good, that's settled then, I'll book a place on the ferry.'

Having done so, I felt quite guilty as the poor chap had just had about six hours of tiring travelling and was just about to face another lot. However, I didn't feel guilty enough to let him off. 'Anyway, there's no point in letting yourself go to waste when you're on leave,' I told him.

We left on the eight o'clock ferry, it wasn't a very good night for lamping really. The moon was up and very little wind. But I was determined to have a night's lamping on some decent land. We shortly arrived at our destination and making myself ready, putting the dogs on their leads, we started on our walk.

We walked field after field and saw very little. What slight breeze there had been, had now completely gone. The night was now the worst there could be for lamping. Having walked about seven miles of the best lamping ground I know, we decided to give up and go back to the van to re-think the situation. We sat in the van chatting for some time and having the occasional cup of tea, which was very welcome, as it was now getting quite cold.

My nephew happened to peer into an old tool box which I kept in the back of my van and found an old hand line and some fishing hooks. 'I've got a brilliant idea,' he announced. 'What about some fishing?' – He was right. A brilliant idea it was, as by now we were getting quite bored and contemplating going home. We had taken some sandwiches with us, so we would use these for bait. There were some very well stocked trout streams not too far from us. So we made haste to the nearest one.

Out of the one hand line we made four smaller ones, and then set off to find ourselves a comfortable place to sit and fish. After a few minutes walking along the stream, I could see the fish rising to the surface to feed. They would make a large ripple on the water which was easy to spot by the light of the moon. I very soon found a good spot baited my line and cast into the middle of the stream. We sat ourselves down and waited. It wasn't two minutes before I had a good strong trout on my line. As I was landing him it reminded me of the year I was poaching almost full time. I was now fishing in the same river. It was plain to see that nothing had changed and it was still just as exciting as it always was.

My nephew had now gone further downstream. No point in us both fishing the same place. I unhooked my fish and cast out again. As soon as the bait hit the water, I baited up my other line and cast that out. By the time that was done it was time to pull in the fist, as another fish was fighting. Again, bait the line and cast and again time to pull in the next line, and so the night went on casting and simply pulling one out. Now and then I would stop what I was doing and pay a visit to my nephew, who was doing just as well, in fact it turned into something of a competition between us.

We decided to finish at about 4.30am in order not to be seen by any early morning Bailiff that might be around. We met at the van about 4.45am and inspected our catch. What a bag! We had forty good size trout, of which I won the contest with over half. We drove off very pleased with our catch, my heart was still pounding with the excitement. We then decided to take a slow drive back in order to catch our ferry back to the Island. We drove down every country lane we could on the way back, looking in the fields. There really was very little about.

As day just broke and we were still looking I could just make out the silhouette of some Roe Deer grazing on the brow of the hill. I pulled the van in some way past the field and made the dogs ready. We walked quietly back along the road and climbed over the gate. The dogs followed and stayed very close, keeping as close to the hedge as possible and walking very slowly uphill.

We were still some distance from the herd, when my nephew stepped on a branch that had fallen from a nearby tree. It made a loud crack as his full weight went on it. I stood motionless… but it was not good, the deer lifted their heads and looked in our direction; they must have detected us in the air – and very soon they were off.

I sent the dogs on, they left us at high speed leaving a trail of dust as they went. We also ran in the same direction. If we were to get a deer we would have to be very quick, it was now getting very light and soon people would be about.

The dogs disappeared over the brow of the hill. We plodded on. It was some time before we got to the top, as it was a fair distance and quite steep. The ground levelled on the top and we could see about a hundred yards to our left there were both dogs with a deer. We ran towards them. I put the dogs quickly back on the leads, my nephew slung the deer over his shoulders and we hurried back to the van. In a very short time we were safely in the van and on our way back to the ferry.

So what stared out to be a total disaster of an evening, turned out to be rather a good one after all.

As we approached the Ferry Terminal, I looked across at my nephew., He was sound asleep, snoring away. No staying-power these young-uns, you know!!!

Too Close for Comfort

The weather had been terrible for quite a few weeks (it seemed like months). There had been very little wind, no drizzle or rain. Plenty of fog and very cold and frosty. No good for lamping at all. I find it very hard to know what to do with myself in such weather. The dogs too get very restless in such conditions. So I walk them as much as I can, but it never seems to satisfy them. They just don't burn up the pent-up energy with a casual walk. So, you can understand my excitement when I heard the wind grow stronger and stronger and the sky become very overcast, enough to threaten rain.

It was a Friday night, so I decided once again to pay a visit to the mainland. There was a new moon on the way, and the nights had been getting lighter, but it looked like it might change tonight. I hurried home from work to pick up my equipment, put my dogs in the van and was off. As the ferry went past Fawley Power Station on its way to Southampton, I could see the smoke from the tall chimney stacks being blown away by the now strong wind. My excitement grew with anticipation of the night to come.

It wasn't long before I was at my lamping ground. I have several places to go lamping on the mainland. This was the smallest place ad usually there is plenty of game to be had. As I left the van, the wind appeared to have dropped a little, but I was still left with a strong breeze, which was acceptable for my purpose. Then I noticed that the sky was beginning to clear, the clouds were breaking up, and a few stars were beginning to show. The light of the moon was penetrating the remaining cloud.

The excitement that I had was now slowly fading. As I could see that the night was going to turn out similar to the past few weeks.

I find it just as interesting to lamp no matter what the weather. It doesn't really upset me if I come home with an empty bag. But having come so far to know that the weather conditions are against you, is very disappointing to say the least.

The first few fields that I walked were reasonably good, and produced four rabbits and plenty of good runs. But it was not long after that that the wind dropped right off and the sky became very light. What a disaster. Any game that was around could hear my approach, in fact could probably even see me coming under normal conditions I would have gone home, but now it was late, the ferries would have stopped running by now and I was too far away from my parent's home to call in and disturb them. I had two choices, either to make myself comfortable in the van and sleep the night out or keep looking in hope that something might turn up.

I took the latter option. I wandered up and down tracks, lanes, and footpaths in vain, there was nothing. I did on one occasion see two fallow dear standing on the edge of a field, as quietly as I could, I crept along the hedgerow in the shadows. But it was obvious they could sense my approach and very soon disappeared out of sight.

I carried on walking where the deer had been. The dogs immediately scented them and made off in the same direction. I knew their efforts would be wasted, as by this time both deer would be far away. I sat down on an old tree stump and waited for the dogs to return.

Whilst waiting I contemplated my next move. The only thing I could think of was to do some fishing. I knew a small fish farm about ten miles away. To go home with some trout was better than nothing.

I set off at once as the night was now getting on. I worked out that by the time I got there I would have about one and a half hours fishing in relative safety, and then it would be time to leave. It never pays to outstay a fishing outing, as they are often well checked throughout the night.

As I drove, I went as many back roads and lanes as possible, stopping periodically and shining the lamp across fields in the hope of finding a herd of grazing deer or even a hare. I drove along one lane and 'What was that?' I saw something shine at the end of the lane. It looked like the beam of a torch. As I approached it disappeared, I carried on driving to where the light had been and stopped the van. I could see nothing. I was sure I hadn't imagined it. Or had I?

I continued driving very slowly along the road, when out of the hedge pounced a man with a torch and two spaniels. Putting the beam from his low powered torch on my face and half blinding my vision, I slid the window open.

'What are you up to?' he asked.

'Why?' I answered.

'Because you've stopped,' he replied.

'Yes,' I said. 'I've stopped because I saw the torch beam as I was driving up the lane.'

'I am the Gamekeeper around here,' he replied, 'and I am looking for poachers after pheasants. My mate's down the road, so you'd better be careful.'

'Be careful of what?' I asked.

'Well if you're thinking about going after pheasants,' he said.

'Thank you very much,' I said. 'Goodbye.'

I drove on rapidly, thinking how close I had come to being caught in pursuit of game, as I had intended to pull in and investigate some fields a little further on. I passed by his mate, whom he had mentioned. I didn't slow down or stop, but drove on as if I hadn't seen him.

Later, after thinking about it, what a stupid keeper he must have been. He gave me all the information I needed, in the fact that he told me who he was, where his mate was, and what was on the land. I thought to myself, if he has that conversation with every potential poacher he meets, I bet he doesn't catch many. Then as an afterthought, maybe he doubles as the village idiot in daytime?

About four or five miles down more roads, I again stopped and peered over a hedge. I scanned the field from right to left, my beam hit directly on a parked up Landrover. My stomach sunk. I quickly outed the light and got back in the van. I had plainly found another gamekeeper. They seemed to be everywhere tonight. I drove off at high speed and never stopped again until I reached the fish farm.

I had made some dough for bait at home, on the off chance that I might do some fishing. A good decision as it turned out, otherwise I would have sat in the van and froze all night.

About half a mile from the farm I parked the van, right by someone's front gate. As to avoid any suspicion from a sharp-eyed passer by noticing a parked van. I kitted myself out with a good size bag to put my catch in and walked along a footpath to the farm. I climbed over a fence and walked over two fields. I could just make out the glistening of the water in the ponds that I intended to fish.

I squeezed through the hedge and then stood and listened for any activity. I could hear the rustling of water from the stream to my left, the coot and moorhen noisily skimming over the water, with the realisation of my presence. That is a very good sign that no one is about, as the birds would have been under cover if anyone else was there.

I felt it was safe to go on. Slowly I walked up a grass bank and noticed that along the ground ran several wires, about a foot ff the ground in height, and about twenty years long. I have seen these before on fish farms. They are the dreaded trip wire. Designed to trip you up, but to pull the fuse on the flare that is attached to either end, is sure to give your game away. If you kick one off there, they light up the entire area. It was lucky for me that the moon was now shining brightly, as I felt sure I would not have noticed them if it had been too dark. I carefully stepped over the wires, crossing about eight in all and running over the ground in different directions.

I had visited this fish farm before when it had just started up. At that time they only had a few ponds, with a few hundred trout in them. But time had been good to the owner, as there were now about eighteen ponds, all containing various weight of fish. It was a job to decide which one to fish first.

I had a good look around the place first as it was possible that someone may have been lurking in some dark corner. I also looked down the approach road to the farm, which leads out on to a main road, and could see that there was a caravan parked on the verges. Nothing unusual about that, most fish farms have one for the night watchmen. This one I fear was for the latter, there was a light on and I could see movement coming from within.

I didn't walk any nearer as the occupier probably had a dog and on such a quiet night it was likely that any dog would hear me. By seeing the light on in the caravan, it helped to make up my mind as to which pond to fish. The answer was obvious – the one nearest to my escape route.

I baited up and started to fish. As the dough hit the water and sank to the bottom, my thoughts went back to narrow escapes I had had in the past, doing just this, and on two occasions actually getting caught.

The penalties if caught are not very severe, a fine and a really good telling off, and perhaps compensation to the owner for any fish taken. In the past I had a partner who was equally keen on night fishing. We would pay a visit to a trout farm and sweep one or two ponds with a long net. One either side of a small pond, drop the net in one end, and both run up to the other end of the pond, dragging the net behind you. The net would get heavier and heavier as we got nearer the end, and finally quickly gathering the net with the catch still in it, then running off with an extremely heavy bag. I was sure that we would drop half our catch in our panic, while making our getaway. I must admit not a very enjoyable way of fishing. But with a greater quantity of fish the rewards were good.

I find fishing with a landline much more challenging and slightly more sporting than with a net. What's more, if you are disturbed it is easy to disregard any line and make your escape without too much fuss.

I was now pulling out fish as fast as I could cast my line and bait up. I had one eye on what I was doing and the other on that caravan door. I could still detect movement coming from inside, so there was no doubt in my mind now – he was the night watchman.

I nearly had all the fish that I wanted, when the inevitable happened. The door of the caravan swung open, and a man with a stick came wandering along in my direction. I gathered my line quickly and stuffed it in my pocket. If I didn't panic, I would have plenty of time. Picking up my fish that I had carefully placed under cover in my bag and making my way towards the hedge, where there was a small ditch, I laid down to watch the still approaching figure.

Within tow or three minutes he was about twenty yards from me and quite oblivious to the fact that he was being watched. He went up and down carefully stepping over the trip wires as he went. He took about fifteen minutes on his rounds. As I lay there my heart was thumping and my adrenalin pumping. I prayed I wouldn't sneeze or anything it would just be my luck for something like that to happen, especially in the night.

It wasn't long before he was on his way back up the track to his nice warm caravan, I waited and watched until he was safely back inside. The door slammed, and all was once again quiet. All I needed was about another half a dozen fish so I threw my line and continued my business. I soon had the number I wanted, and the town church clock struck four o'clock. It was time to go. Gathering my things and making my way back to the van.

I drove off in search of other prey, again stopping now and again to peer over a hedge. But there was nothing – no rabbit, hare or deer.

Taking a slow drive back to the Southampton Ferry Port, and waiting my time for the first ferry back to the Island. This I did. Parking in the appropriate place, I curled up on the front seat and had an hour's kip. The next think I heard was 'Got your ticket mate?' Giving the collector my ticket, I was homeward bound.

A very disappointing night. I had one too many conversations with gamekeepers and too many night-watchmen about. When I am out, I don't really like to see anyone, friend or foe. I feel the night is for me ONLY and is not to be shared with OTHERS.

Hedging

This time of the year is beautiful, especially in early morning. It is the end of November and early morning fields are white with a thick carpet of frost. Most of the Autumn leaves have fallen from the trees, the long grass is fast dying down and the hedgerows are becoming bare and empty.

I find myself leaving home as early as I can on such mornings, with my dogs for company, to wander up and down the fields and hedgerows in search of rabbits which have not gone to ground, but decided to take refuge in thick undergrowth, I find this the best time for these outings. Preferably if there should be a slight breeze. I can't really say why, but have always found that there is much more to be had on such days. The fields are only about five minutes from where I live and I usually take all my dogs along with me, as it is usually just a half-hearted hunting trip.

I have two small dogs, one is a very small Border Collie and the other is a small Mongrel, which looks like a stunted Golden Retriever. He stands about sixteen inches high. Neither of these dogs are much good for anything in particular as they were bought just as pets. But as luck would have it, about two years ago they both decided that they loved noting better than running through the middle of hedgerows finding rabbits. So, a good semi working relationship was made between them and the lurchers. As the dogs work their way up a hedgerow the lurchers stay outside waiting for the screams and barks of excitement from the dogs on the scent of a rabbit.

Usually I stand well back and let them get on with it. It is very interesting to watch, the lurchers place themselves in what they consider to be the most likely place for the rabbit to break cover, the excitement and alertness on their faces is good to see. It isn't long before one can hear the dogs in the hedge beat their way at high speed up the line of hedge and push out a rabbit. Immediately the lurchers are about their work. A good easily seen course and the rabbit usually caught in next to no time. After such an event I make a big fuss of all my dogs and then back to work for another.

Belle my best lurcher has become very good at this method of hunting and experience has taught her that sometimes a rabbit will make its way a considerable distance up the hedgerow before breaking cover. She then leaves us and goes further up, finds a suitable entrance into the hedge and stands and waits. More times than not a rabbit will run straight into her path, she catches it in the hedge and proudly brings it out and returns it to me.

On other occasions when she thinks the changes of that are low, she walks on the opposite side of the hedge to me. She seems to realise that with my talking to the other dogs if a rabbit is going to come out, it would be likely to go away from me, toward Belle. These things I consider to be very clever for she has never been trained to do them. It has got to be the hunting instinct she was born with. I am lucky to have such a dog.

Meg my other lurcher has different ideas. She tends to stay level with the dogs in the hedge but way out in the field about three metres or more. When a rabbit breaks cover, she has plenty of time to see which way he is headed and can take appropriate action. On a number of occasions, she can beat Belle to the catch, as sometimes she and the rabbit are running toward one another. However, she, I feel, has never got her mind completely on her job, as if there are very few noises coming out of the hedge with the dogs n the scent of a rabbit, or if few rabbits have been found, she will wander further and further away from us and go and look for her own in some long grass somewhere, she still has a lot to learn. But she tries hard to please.

Left Behind

Whilst cleaning the dog kennels out one day, I was called away by the telephone ringing. In my panic to get to the phone before it stopped, I forgot to close the kennel door. On my return I didn't take long to discover that all five dogs had one. I was astounded at the speed in which they had disappeared. I ran down to the road, but no sign of them, so I got in my van and drove up and down the road, still nothing. The last thing I could think of was, that maybe they were wander around over at the farm. So, to the farm where I walked and called – nothing. I was on the brink of going home to wait for their return, when I heard a bark in the distance. The bark was that of my Border Collie. Very soon I traced their whereabouts and stood and watched. The collie and the mongrel noisily exploring through the hedge, and the lurchers well placed on the outside. I watched for some time until a rabbit broke cover and made a dash into the open field. Meg started after him, followed very closely by Belle. All of a sudden the rabbit turned and Belle was there. I waited some more to see what would be done with the said rabbit. Belle twisted and turned to prevent the other dogs getting a hold on her catch. All the dogs were now gathered round. Belle made a sudden break and headed homeward., Just as she passed, I showed myself and called her. Her tail wagged as she came to me and handed over the rabbit. It was a wonderful sight to see all five dogs working together as a small pack, especially when they had a catch. But a strange feeling came over me with the realisation that maybe I wasn't needed any more, or even worse – Just not welcome.

Belle's young pup is eight months old now, I am still not working her with any regularity as I want her bones to grow strong first. I take her with me on such walks, it is extremely good practice for young pups, it keeps them alert and helps them to be aware of what is being caught. It has other bonuses such as helping a young pup to find out about getting through or under wire fences and finding their way through or under wire fences and finding their way through hedges etc. Plus, of course, the reasonably steady but vital exercise they receive is essential for a growing pup.

Hare and Dog Give Up

The Isle of Wight Coursing Club had a meet on November 26th at 1.30 in the afternoon. I was very keen to attend as I have only had the chance to go once this season. The ground was very dry, not particularly hard which was surprising owing to the amount of hard frosts we have had lately. But overall the ground was good for an afternoon's coursing.

It wasn't a very good turnout of people with dogs. In fact, most of the people who brought along their Greyhounds seemed to want to save their dog's energy for coursing on the Mainland. There were about six Greyhounds that were usually put up for a course and about eight lurchers.

The first field walked was empty, not a hare in sight and although it was only a small field, some walkers looked quite miserable. I heard one say to another 'it looks to be another disastrous week'. 'Yes,' came the reply. 'Funny though, it was good down here last year.'

As soon as we entered the next field lined up and started walking down. Up came our first hare. A good strong looking hare he was too. He made off after being given a good start with the first two Greyhounds to course close on his tail. It didn't last very long as the Har managed to outwit (which wasn't very hard) both greyhounds, the owners of the two dogs disappeared over a hedge to collect their dogs. It never ceases to amaze me how many people have to actually fetch their dogs after a course. There aren't too many greyhounds with the sense to return to their master after a run. Two new dogs were then placed in the slip, and on we walked, nothing more to be found in that field. But on to the next.

The ground was easy walking, the newly planted seed was now sprouting to two inches high, which although was think in places seemed to bind the topsoil together making the walking pleasant.

The next field was the best I had seen for Hares in the daytime for ages. The first course came after about two minutes walking and the two greyhounds in the slips were released. They both sped off after the hare. The course was a good one and very easily seen. All the action was directly in front of us, it was a good sight. Although the dogs were plainly wearing the Hare down, they were getting nearer and nearer to a half-grown hedge with barbed wire running through the middle. The hare was turned once more by the stronger of the two dogs and then made straight for the hedge. The dogs had lost a little ground by this time but were starting to close in once more. The hare, on reaching the line of hedge promptly disappeared out of sight. The dogs took the gamble that the hare went straight through and continued on the other side. As the first dog approached the hedge, he took a good high jump in order to clear the oncoming obstacle, this he did very successfully and continued to curse his way into the next field. The second dog however, was not so lucky. As he approached the hedge, he obviously misjudged his distance and hooked his foreleg on the barbed wire, ripping down the side of his leg, causing a very severe injury. This was witnessed by all, including the owner. A few rushed over to the dog, which was by now standing a short distance away on the other side of the hedge. The greyhound had completely torn out a muscle in his leg and at this stage it was plain to see, he would never run again.

We carried him back to a now waiting van on what turned out to be his last journey – (to the Vet).

The next to dogs to run were lurchers, one was a Saluki X Greyhound, the other was Belle – my dog. As the two dogs sped off the hare headed slightly uphill away from us and disappeared out of sight. Both dogs followed, it was another minute before all three were sighted some way in the distance. We stood and watched a very good course. Up and down and up and down again they went, until it was just visible to see one dog break off and head back towards us, it was Belle, she had obviously had quite enough of chasing this very strong hare up and down.

The other dog however carried on. Both hare and dog would come and go out of sight, only to reappear in a totally different field and still going just as strong. As they disappeared behind the last hill the owner decided to take a walk in the same direction to retrieve his dog, when he got to the point of sighting both dog and hare, still going, he could see that they were both worn out. They were both going at a snail's pace, neither could hardly move a muscle. He watched as the hare literally crawled into a nearby ditch and come to a stop. The lurcher was just as tired as he followed and lay down a few feet from the panting hare. Both dog and hare had given up. They lay there for some time just looking around them trying to regain strength to carry on.

The owner of the dog quickly fastened a collar and lead on the dog and stood with him until he had the strength to walk back to the still waiting group. The hare didn't even have the strength to move, when a large man stood over it. It was completely sapped of its strength, but would recover in a very short time.

Owner and dog re-joined us and carried on walking with the rest of us. The hare being left to run another day, he did so well and deserved his freedom.

The afternoon went on, we all had more than enough hares to run our dogs on It was a good afternoon's coursing. But shadows caused by the sad end of a good greyhound.

A Sunday Afternoon's Run

A boring Sunday afternoon, sitting around not quite knowing what to do with myself, when I suddenly had an idea. There is a certain area of land on a farm not too far from my home which I had been meaning to take a look at in daylight hours.

The land itself has plenty of game living on it and although I have paid several visits to it at night the owner just will not give permission for any hunting whatsoever to take place.

On travelling past the said land in a car, one can see quite many pheasants feeding along the hedgerows. At night there are always plenty of hares and rabbits to be taken.

The farmer is a large man who took the farm on about two years ago. Most of the farm work he does himself, but I have noticed of late that he is employing a couple of labourers. What also appears to be the farmer's favourite pastime is shooting. He seems to think that he has sole rights to the birds that fly and the rabbits and hares that run through his land. Personally, I will not accept this attitude as I believe such animals were put on the earth for all, not a select few.

On the few occasions that I have asked for permission, the first being over the telephone and the second being a personal visit to him. When I asked as politely as I could, having recited my words prior to my arrival at his door, and even offered a small amount of payment for the privilege of hunting his land. The answers he gave me one can only describe as 'downright rude'. Quite unrepeatable in this book, or in any pleasant company.

I cannot for the life of me understand such a reaction, unfortunately it happens only too often and makes one come away felling quite sick. A message to such type of farmers s obvious. Manners will cost you nothing, A simple 'Yes' or 'No' will do. My reaction when I have been spoken to in such a way is – this chap obviously has something to hide on his land the thought of anyone else seeing or finding it is too much for him to bear. My thoughts then say 'Let's have a look'.

So back to the story. I left home with the idea of having a good look around on the land. Pulling up around half a mile away from my entry on to the land and took a slow walk. Walking the best part of the way to the land through a neighbouring wood. I could see there were some pheasants around, running and ducking under cover as I approached. As I broke from the wood, I found myself at the edge of the land which I intended to look over. I hopped over the fence and walked some more, up and down the hedges, and in and out of the woods, I was right. Partridge, pheasant and hares were in good numbers. Everywhere I looked there was something on the move. Having walked about two miles I noticed a hide built out of straw bails a few yards out from a hedge. Standing back against a hedge I crouched down for a while and waited, wondering if anyone was inside. After about half an hour I took a gamble that all was okay. Slowly approaching, being very careful not to make any noise or sudden movement, at this stage I didn't want to be detected.

Finally, I reached the hide and peered in over the top. A sigh of relief came as I could see my hunch was right – Empty. Looking around the outside there were the inevitable empty gun cartridges and a pile of around sixty pigeons. I stuck my and inside the pile and they were warm. Looking further out into the field I counted another five shot pheasants. Picking up the nearest one it too was warm. Whoever had shot them hadn't been gone very long and I wondered if they could have been watching me now. Slowly walking back to the hedge, I got behind some thick undergrowth and scanned the line of fields and hedges in front of me. I felt reasonably sure there was no one around. Waiting until I could wait no more, I took a length of string from my pocket and made a quick dash to the dead pheasants and quickly gathering them up and tying them with the string, I started to make my way back the way I had come – only quicker. Just a short distance to go, when looking to my left to the top of the field, I could see a large man running in my direction, shouting and waving a large stick. My stomach sunk. I stood for a second to get my bearings for a quick getaway. There was only one option, over a barbed wire fence and down into a wood. Slinging the pheasants over my shoulder I made off. Running as hard as I could I took a quick glance behind me. 'Blimey' he was gaining on me. By this time my heart was pumping really fast, but I had entered the wood and tried to lose him by running left and right. Then I took a short rest, but could hear him beating his way through the thick wood. Panic was now setting in, which doesn't help one to think straight. I ran again until a sudden stop brought me to a very muddy stream. This was familiar to me and it had to be crossed. So, in I jumped and sank in the thick smelly mud, made my way to the other side to try and regain my breath and thoughts. The farmer was still coming. At this time, I considered myself to be reasonably safe, as I felt sure he wouldn't cross the stream. Setting off once more I now headed slightly uphill, deeper into the heart of the wood. Stopping after another ten minutes or so to listen. I could hardly believe it. He was still coming. It was time to take some serious action!

I released the pheasants from my string, thinking that maybe if he found them it might take his mid off the chase. Then hurriedly made my way back walking in a semi-circle to avoid bumping into my pursuer. I walked as quietly as possible as I could still hear him beating through. But the sounds seemed to be getting further and further away. Hurrying on even faster I was very soon back over the stream and out of the wood. Jumping over the fence back into the fields, I saw lying on the ground his large stick and a hat. Going over to them I pushed the stick firmly into the soil and stuck the hat on top of the stick. Just to let him know that I had been there and he had been outwitted.

Making my way back to the car, arms and legs and chest aching with all the running, I vowed never to return again. Well – not in day time anyway!

Sacked on The Spot

Another very popular and very profitable method of earning money as a lad was to work on the Farms in the summer holidays. Getting in the bales of straw and hay from the fields was commonly known as bale-carting.

The pay once again was extremely good for a fit, strong lad who was willing to put in long hours. The idea was that after the Combine Harvester had been along a few days earlier, and thrashed all the ripe seed from the crop, and then left the remaining straw or hay in neatly tied and cut bales, the local lads would come around, pick up these bales and stack them neatly in a vacant barn.

The work itself was very hard and more times than not the weather was very warm. It wasn't long before one could work up a right old sweat. Also, some of the straw flakes were very sharp and could work their way firmly into your skin, setting in a very nasty rash and sometimes stinging little cuts that would irritate for weeks afterwards.

The business was usually done by the amount of bales actually stacked in the barn. At the time I think it was about 3d a bale. Sometimes it would be done on time, i.e. so much per day, but this was quite unusual.

One summer, a friend and I applied for such a job and felt lucky being taken on straight away, to join a small team of men and boys. We were very soon organised and well into our work. It was estimated that there would be two- or three-weeks work bale-carting for this estate.

The farm that we were working on that belonged to the estate was a very well-kept place. Beautiful farm houses and relatively clean and tidy as far as farmyards go. The place itself had obviously had a great deal of money recently spent on it as there were brand new outhouses, and new tractor lean-to type sheds all over the place.

On one particular lunch break I enquired as to why apparently no expense had been spared on this farm when some of the other farms on this estate look run down and shabby.

'I don't really know,' came the reply from the farmhand in charge. 'The owner just seems to like this place best,' he said. 'Especially now he's got his prize bull that he's just paid thousands for, in the brand-new bull pen.'

This comment got my interest up immediately.

'Can I have a look?' I asked.

'Sure', came the reply. 'follow me I'll show you.' As we peered over the high wall that surrounded the bull, I was speechless. He sure was a magnificent beast. He was massive and rippling muscles flanked his body with a great big neck and very deep pounding chest. His beauty was breath-taking. One could almost sense the power that was in him. I spent some time just looking at him shuffling around his pen. 'Yes' I thought, 'he was beautiful indeed.'

The shout for work soon awoke me from my trance. I wandered back to the men waiting for me to join them, and then all of a sudden I became excited as I realised that at long last it was my turn to drive the tractor.

To drive the tractor was an honour indeed, and regarded as an easy time. Certainly a bit of rest from stacking and moving bales of straw and hay into the barn. A real feeling of happiness came over me as I would be driver for at least the next few days. All I had to do was to drive the tractor to the fields, reverse into the small stacks of straw that were dotted around the field, shut the vice-like clamps that were attached to the back of the tractor, pick them up and away. These small stacks contained about twelve bales each. They had been previously stacked by hand which made things a lot easier for the tractor driver who could readily just drive up, collect them, and return them straight away to the men waiting to stack them into the barn.

We were soon well and truly back in the swing of things after our well-deserved dinner break. I was collecting bales and returning them to the barn nearly as fast as the men could stack them. Field after field was soon becoming empty and we had a quick discussion about how much longer we intended to work, when it was very soon agreed on another two loads – that is twenty-four bales, would do for the day as we would have another early start in the morning.

I set off on my penultimate journey, backed up, clamps on, lift and away. As I started my return, I spotted one bale sitting all on its own in the middle of the field. It was obviously one that had dropped from the top of a stack on some previous journey. So I decided to pick it up on my way. I veered off and headed in its direction, stopping nearby, and jumping down from the seat of the cab. I grasped the bale with both hands and with a good strong push the bale landed right on top of the stack that I had on board and so back into the cab to complete my journey.

After a few minutes I arrived back at the farm. I pulled into the yard and as I started to climb up a small bank to go round to the barn I felt the steering of the tractor become very easy. In fact, the steering wheel was totally out of control and no matter which way I steered the tractor went completely its own way. It was a nightmare as I could do nothing but just sit and watch. My brain was too slow in telling my feet to brake. I went into blind panic!!!

The tractor veered gracefully to the left, I suppose at a speed of about 20 mph Absolute shock horror came over me when I saw what I was now headed for. Yes, you've guessed it, the brand-new Bull Pen, containing the pedigree bull – a prize one at that! I was powerless, I sat back and watched as the front of the tractor careered through the side of the pen and slowly jolted to a halt.

After all the dust and debris had settled, even more shock hit me as the bull was squashed between the frame of the tractor and the far wall. He was snorting and kicking and in general making a lot of funny noises. As he tried to get free, the now still tractor was rocking to and fro. I remember looking into his face (the bull), his eyes were bulging out of his head. I don't know whether it was fright or rage but he sure didn't look very happy.

I got my senses together and made a quick scramble out of the back of the tractor, over the bales and ran around to the barn. On approaching it the man in charge said 'Where have you been? We thought you'd got lost or something.'

'Nothing like that,' I said. 'I've had a bit of an accident with the tractor.'

'Oh my god,' he said, 'what have you done?'

I replied, 'well, you know the new bull Pen, well I've just knocked a hole it with the tractor'

'Oh, no,' he said, 'the Guvnor will go mad, how big is the hole? Can you put your hand through it?' he asked.

'I should think so,' I said, 'the tractor is parked in there!'

As he ran around the corner to have a look, the rest of us slowly followed. When we arrived at the scene there he was stood absolutely motionless, mouth wide open and quite quite speechless. His colour? Well it was white, or was it green? Some funny colour anyway. He finally pulled himself together enough to mumble something about going to get the Guvnor and took a slow shuffle up to the large house.

We all stood about wondering what we should do. The only noises that were being made were coming from the other side of the wall. I peered around the corner and there was my old mate the bull looking angrier than ever but was showing clear signs of exhaustion.

A few minutes had past when I heard a door slam hard, and across the yard came the Guvnor marching at high speed, straight toward me. He did look upset!

'You stupid bastard!' was his greeting to me. I remember it well. 'I'm going to tell you something son,' he said, 'you – are – a – stupid – bastard,' he said, poking me in the chest as he went. Turning to his man-in-charge he said 'How much do we owe him for his work?'

Thirty pounds was the answer and digging into his pockets the Guvnor pulled out a wad of notes. Dealing off thirty pounds exactly he slapped them into my hand.

Hmm, no tip? I thought.

'Now get off my property,' he said, 'and never ever let me see you here again, go on, be off with you.'

'I'm going, I'm going,' I said, and went home with my tail between my lets feeling kind of sad that I had lost my good job. Isn't it funny that some people just have no sense of humour, have they?

Easy Money

One last story of earning pocket money as a young lad was on one holiday break from school when I decided to take a nice long bicycle ride to a little village about ten miles from where I lived. A good school friend lived in this particular village and it was him I intended to visit.

After a hard journey I finally arrived at his house, leaned my bike on the garden fence and made my way up the path to the door. I gave three knocks on the large oak door. After a short time, a very plump middle-aged lady answered and as I looked down, she was surrounded by about seven small children, all different sizes and shapes. But the funny thing was they all had the very distinctive round faces with very rosy cheeks and little button noses, which could only belong to the Brown family. Somewhere around I thought to myself there are another seven children. They were a very large family of fourteen children. As hard as I tried, I couldn't see the missing seven. Maybe they were hiding from me behind the hedge that ran alongside the house, or maybe they were peering from the windows carefully hidden by the hanging curtains? My eyes carefully scanned every nook and cranny hoping to spot one or two.

Mrs Brown must have wondered what the hell I was playing at, 'Have you lost something?' she asked.

'Err, no,' I replied. 'I've come to see Tim, Mrs Brown, is he in?'

'Wait here a minute I'll go and have a look.' She disappeared into the darkness of the long hall, which left me stood on the doorstep being watched eagerly by seven pairs of eyes. All the children looked me up and down and one ventured out and walked around the back of me, to see I suppose if I looked the same as everyone else does from the back! A very little girl came forward towards me, hit me on the leg, and promptly ran back indoors. I had a strange feeling that I was being watched from behind, so I spun around on my heels and sure enough, another three Browns had come out of the woodwork to inspect the stranger standing on the doorstep. The unusual thing was that, not one of them said anything, not a word, they just stood and stared.

Come on Tim, come on Tim, I thought to myself. At long last I could hear footsteps re-approaching down the hall. As a figure came into sight, I could see it wasn't Tim, but Mrs Brown again.

'He ain't in,' she exclaimed.

'Oh, any idea where I might find him?' I asked.

'No, he could be up on the farm, down the cress beds, or over the fields, I don't know,' she said.

'Well if I don't find him will you tell him I called? Thank you, bye,' I replied.

I made a very brisk walk back to my bike, mounted and peddled off as fast as I could. I got around the corner, out of sight of the Brown's house, and took a breather. Blimey, I thought to myself, they were a strange lot, for a horrible moment there I thought they were sizing me up to eat, or something just as sinister!

I wandered over local fields, up and down roads and anywhere else I could think of where I might find Tim. It was just about when I was to give up looking, when I spotted the lonely figure of a young lad walking towards me on the road. I waited until he got close and very soon the figure became clear enough to see that it was indeed, Tim. Once again, I mounted my bike and sped off to meet hm.

We made our greetings on meeting each other and sat on the grass verge of the road and had a chat. It was then that

Tim explained what exactly he had been up to that afternoon. He had, in fact, been to one of the local farms, shooting with a .22 Air Rifle. His quarry had been rats and pigeons. The farmer whose farm it belonged to had some weeks before offered 3d for each rat shot and 6d per pigeon to Tim, and form what I could gather it was a free-for-all with the local lads. Just about anyone was welcome who had a gun.

By the end of the week I was equipped with a very good gun that belonged to another friend of mine, who offered to lend it to me, for a fiver.

The very next weekend I set off once more to meet Tim. I had arranged to meet him at the farmer's house, early in the morning, where he would introduce me to the farmer an get his permission to shoot. This was very soon granted and into the farmyard we went.

First of all, we decided that the best plan of action was to search all the barns, buildings and outhouses, and that the quieter we were, obviously the more we would shoot. We discussed that we should each visit a number of buildings and return to the start on completion.

Off we went on our separate ways. I quickly entered the first building, which was in fact an old-fashioned milking parlour. I stood quietly for a few minutes looking around. At that time, I couldn't see any rats at all but I could sure hear them scuffling around the floor above. I decided to go further into the building and investigate ways of getting upstairs. I slowly walked down the narrow passage and along dust-ridden spiders' webs, which brushed up against my face as I went. The parlour had obviously not been used for years. I approached the end of the passage and turned left, and there in front of me was a rather dangerous and unsafe looking narrow staircase leading to the old grain store upstairs. Gingerly, I trod up the stairs and on reaching the top, I slowly peered around the floor. My eyes were just about level with the floor so I had a very good view of anything moving around, and sure enough there was plenty to be seen. There were large rats, small rats, brown and black rats, some were sat on their haunches nibbling bits of grain, some were gnawing on wood, and I spotted some fighting with any other rat they could find. I just stood and watched for a few minutes, I had never in my life seen so many rats in one place. The farmer who owned the property needed a lot more than local lads with air rifles, perhaps the Pied Piper of Hamelin would do, I thought!

I carefully aimed at the nearest rat to me and fired getting a direct hit. The rat jumped into the air slightly as the slug made contact, and on landing rolled on its side and lay perfectly still. Quite a few remaining rats scattered away quickly at the sound of the blast.

I quickly re-loaded and looked for another rat. I could just make out the silhouette of one sitting up on one of the many beams that ran overhead. Again, I took aim and fired. Another hit, he fell from the beam and landed with a thud on the wooden floor.

I was really starting to get into this now and at a rough estimate I was killing about three rats every ten minutes. I missed quite a few owing to the bad light in the building.

Tim had told me before we stared, to bring a pair of gloves to pick up the dead with. He went on to say that they were so full of germs and disease that people have become very sick indeed from handling farm rats, and in fact, some have even died. I pulled the thick leather glove that I had brought with me, over my hand, and made my way up the last remaining steps to the floor, walked over and collected the dead rats. I threw them down the staircase and on to the floor below. Not a bad shoot, I thought, as I went. Twelve in all.

After descending the stairs and placing the rats in a newest pile to be collected later in the day, I made my way to the next building. There were many more rats that were shot by us on our first circuit of the buildings. As I remember, we scored a grand total of forty by mid-afternoon.

We decided at that time to give the rat shooting a rest and give the pigeons a good thinning out, until it was time to go home. The pigeons were not around in such great numbers as the rats, but a good score was bagged, with the fact that a lot of the birds bagged were stray tame ones, which enabled us to get close enough to get a good shot. We managed to get a total of twelve pigeons by the time we were ready to go home. It was a very enjoyable and exciting day. All that remained was to take the bag to the farmer and be rewarded for our day's work. The farmer seemed pleased with s and invited us back whenever we wanted.

'Right,' said Tim as we left the farmyard. 'Time to go, do you fancy coming back with me for some tea or something?'

'Err, no I don't think so Tim, thanks all the same, but its late and I really should be getting back home now,' I said, remembering all those eyes watching me before. I went away down the road on my bike feeling very satisfied with my days' work, and even more pleased that I resisted the temptation of going back to the Brown's for tea… or something! Just maybe it was me they had planned for their tea!!!

Birds of Prey

In the past, as a youngster, I spent quite a lot of time with Birds of Prey. What wonderful specimens of the animal world they are. I am very out of touch with the law on owning such birds now, but in my day, they were very easy to obtain legally or otherwise. Never did I consider myself an expert with the handling and training of the birds, but they gave me a great deal of pleasure when I kept them ,never was I into the big time so to speak, and collect the very rare and expensive birds, I would stick to the more accessible, such as sparrow hawks, kestrels, and buzzards, doing my very best with the long job of training such birds and there was always plenty of information on such matters in the local library.

One of my major faults was, as is with most youngsters, my impatience. I would spend hours and hours feeding, tending and training my birds, and then before they were properly trained, would take them to some far-off field to fly them, where I would stand and watch them fly gracefully into the far-off distance never to be seen again!

Most of the birds I owned cost between thirty to sixty pounds, depending on the breed. On one occasion I purchased a beautiful male Common Buzzard. It was the first of its kind that I had kept, and I remember being beside myself with excitement on the day of its arrival at the local train station. After picking it up and signing the appropriate papers as proof of its safe arrival, I drove it home at breakneck speed to inspect the new addition to my collection.

The Buzzard was kept at the bottom of our very long garden on a well-made bow perch, and over the top was a beautifully built shelter against the weather. There was not expense spared when it came to accommodation. Our back garden unfortunately adjoined another with belonged to two rather old ladies and on noticing the presence of such a fierce looking bird, we very soon received reports that they were both scared stiff to venture into their garden for fear of such a savage bird flying at them. 'What a load of rubbish!' I remember thinking to myself and in any case these birds go for meat – not bone! However, the bird was very soon moved out of their sight, further down the garden. Not too far from the bird's perch was a shallow pool of water, made from the bottom five inches of a forty-gallon drum. This proved to be very successful, as both drinking and bathing water, these birds are extremely clean and love nothing more than a good bath in nice clean water, and afterward spending a great deal of time grooming themselves and keeping their flight feathers in tip top condition.

The next problem of the new location of the bird soon followed. My father was a very keen keeper of Bantams. At the time it seemed that nothing was more sacred than his birds, (apart from my mother, of course). The Bantams would roam the top half of the garden forever scratching around in the soil for food. They all seemed very happy with their lot. Until one day, one of the Bantams discovered that there was an ample supply of water not too far from home. So, venturing forth to sample the new drinking supply, he found that he had ventured a little too near to the strange looking bird that stood on a stick all day long.

As the evening feed time came for the Buzzard, the dreadful truth dawned. As I approached there were feathers everywhere. I went into what can only be described as deep shock, and panic. Looking back towards the house I could see that my dad had arrived back from work, his car was parked in the drive. The terrible fact was that he would soon be along to feed his birds, and he was bund to notice that one was missing. Dashing along to our small shed, I managed to find a small plastic bag, just right to put feathers in, and then acting very fast and furiously picking up the feathers, managed to hide all traces of the day's events.

My father by now had decided the time was right to feed his birds and was approaching at speed. My mind raced to find some sort of diversion. The only thing I could think of was to go and have a lengthy chat with him. This I did, the questions came thick and fast.

'What sort of a day did you have Dad?'

'What did you make today Dad?'

'Hasn't it been a nice day, Dad?'

He looked at me puzzled and said, 'Haven't you got anything to do?'

Giving up I walked away, but I hung around, not too close and kept an eye on what was going on. My luck held as he finished the feeding and happily walked back indoors for his tea.

'See you later, Nipper,' he said as he went.

So far, I had got away with it, so I sighed a breath of relief, and got on with my jobs.

Unfortunately, that wasn't the end of it. The same thing happened on three more occasions over the next few days. The last time it was my father who found the half-eaten carcase of one of his best layers. Again, the Buzzard had to be moved, coming to rest in a far corner of the garden completely out of harm's way. (I thought).

Arriving back from work early one evening, I prepared the food for my bird, which consisted of frozen day-old chicks, bred for the purpose of feeding such birds of prey (a change from Bantams, I suppose). However, I then walked to the end of the garden to feed him. Shock and horror hit me as I arrived at the perch. No bird was there to greet me – he had gone! The line and Jesse were still there, but the Buzzard was nowhere to be seen.

For a long time I searched high and low, up and down the road, looking in everyone's gardens. I couldn't understand how on earth he had made his getaway so clean. On returning home I inspected the line and Jessies, but they were all in perfect condition. The only reason for hm getting loose, as far as I could see, was that someone had set him free. (I wonder if it was my dad). I carried my search on for the rest of the evening, and a good part of the next day, but to no avail. Finally, I gave up and got back to a more normal way of living, for want of a better phrase.

Around about ten days after, while at home one evening, the telephone rang; answering, a voice on the other end said, 'Hello, it's the local Police Station here. Do you still keep Birds of Prey?'

'Yes, I replied. 'Why do you ask?'

'Because just down the road from the station in a tall tree there is a very hungry looking Buzzard. Anything to do with you?'

'Yes, I said. 'Would you please catch it for me and I'll come straight along.'

'Not bloody likely!' came the answer. 'These birds are dangerous you know!'

Funny statement to make, I thought, they must have been talking to the old ladies next door.

Leaving home, I proceeded to eat the rest of my tea as I went it was only a few minutes before – as the Police would say – At The Scene. Sure enough there was my Buzzard sitting on the uppermost branches of a tree. It took a very long, slow, and difficult climb to the top. I could see by looking at him, he had had something of a hard time. As he became at arms-length from me, he ventured forward as if to jump on my hand. I propped myself on to one of the heavier limbs and called him. To my surprise he hopped straight on to my hand

and immediately gave an affectionate nip with his beak. (If indeed there is such a thing from a Buzzard).

Then I had to negotiate the long climb down. There was quite an audience by now, had come to watch the situation which was becoming quite embarrassing to say the least. Finally making it safely down barring a few holes made in my arm, caused by the razor-sharp talons of the bird's feet, and after giving a short speech on the eating habits and training of Birds of Prey to the astonished crowd that had built up, I made my way home. Placing the bird back on his perch and giving him a really good feed, which he much appreciated. I made up my mind he had to go. I would find something easier to handle and perhaps something that would get along with little old ladies. This would be hard to find. I thought what about a Budgie?

Pheasants

As we all know the pheasant is one of the most sought-after birds in game season, in fact, most of the game season is hinged on this very bird. Never have I really made a habit to catch or poach these birds, but I suppose in the past I have had my fair share. There are so many ways of catching pheasants that the poacher is quite spoilt for choice. Myself, I would use the easiest and quickest methods which are available.

On a nearby shoot, where I once lived, there were many birds. The area itself was heavy wooded country. The woods themselves were the place where most Pheasants could be had. In each small wood the gamekeeper had set out release pens. Just before the start of the shooting season, the pheasants which had been reared in the pens were released to roam free. The keeper's job was then to carry on feeding the birds to keep them local, or at least, until the beaters would come and put the birds into flight for shooting.

In between the time of the birds being released and the shoot starting, the birds are very tame. Any human being that comes within eyeshot they crowd around hoping to be fed. So, on such occasions when I knew the keeper was not around, I would arm myself with an air pistol, or even better, a catapult. Both were very effective and a good bag could be had very quickly with the minimum of fuss. Another simple method was to encourage the birds away with food, to some place where the risk of being detected was less. Once you have the birds feeding where you want them, the rest is relatively easy.

Spread your corn down amongst the grass, make a hole in the ground about six to seven inches deep and about three inches in diameter, again put down some more corn, then set an ordinary rabbit wire over the top of the hole, but with a slightly smaller diameter, about two and a half inches will do. Put down yet more corn, and an extra amount down the hole. Sooner or later your pheasants will eagerly eat all the corn they can see. They will then see the corn down the hole and attempt to get at it, placing their long neck down through the mesh wire to reach the food. It is not until they try to withdraw their head, that they are truly caught. This is an excellent method of catching pheasants with very little risk. However, beware when you go to collect your bag, someone may be watching!

The next method is one of the most popular and on a good night brings the best results. That is – Shooting the Roosting Pheasants.

After a long day's mooching around for food, pheasants retire to the woods to roost. They fly up into the lower branches of the trees and stay for the night. The best night to operate this method is on a windy moonlight night. On entering a wood where pheasants are to be found, place yourself under the branches of the trees and simply look up. The dark silhouette of the roosting pheasants shows up well against the moonlight night. All that remains is to take aim and fire with a silent gun. If the wind is not strong enough, you will find yourself in trouble. As the pheasants and pigeons that are roosting will leave the trees, making what appears to be a deafening noise and really giving the game away to some wary gamekeeper. If the moon is not up it is hard to see the roosting birds as everything is so dark. But a torch will suffice, a quick flash with the beam can be seen a long way off. So as soon as you have a few from one area, it pays to move off to another. The last method I wat to tell about is back again to the rabbit snare.

As the pheasants leave the fields and open spaces at dusk and start their journey to the woods for their night's roost, they invariably have to walk under wire fences and through hedges. If one sits and watches for a few nights, it is easy to learn exactly where the birds are walking through All that remains then, is to set your snares at the right height – go home - returning back after dark will reveal your catch.

All these methods of pheasant poaching are very successful, but one must need to keep a wary eye open for keepers that may have discovered what you are about. If you have pheasants in a snare which the keeper has spotted, he has time on his side and can sit and wait for you to return. What is even worse is, that he may well have a friend or two with him, in the shape of the Local Police Force.

Only once have I been seen by a keeper collecting my catch from some nares. He sat and waited for my return one night, some distance away from where the pheasant lay. The keeper himself wasn't very bright. Most of the local lads knew his Landrover, including me, and could easily avoid him. On my return to collect any catch I might have I would always go by the most unexpected route that I could find, i.e. through thick undergrowth, or through rivers if available.

On one occasion I was stumbling through a really thick wood when I came upon the keeper's Land Rover. It was hidden, but parked under the trees which lined a small discussed track. Waiting for any sign of movement for as long as time I could spare. I ventured forth as quietly as possible.

Th night was drawing in quite quickly now and it wouldn't be too long before I was unable to see what I was doing. It was just then I spotted the keeper sitting on a tree stump facing a very clear view of my rabbit wires containing eight pheasants. I stood for a time stunned by what I saw, then quickly and quietly back-tracked on myself and headed for my birds in another direction, Minutes later I was just approaching my catch, I could make out the dark silhouette of the hanging birds. At the far end of the lie was a bird that had been caught but was still on its feet and very lively – what was I to do? Should I go and get the live one first? Kill him and get the others, or collect the seven dead ones and leave the live one til last? Lessening the risk of any noise the bird might make while being killed. Deciding on the latter, I crawled along the ground on my belly, taking the birds out of the wires as I went. I considered I was doing really well, having a good advantage over the keeper, as I knew where he was and he didn't know where I was. That is until I approached the live pheasant. I was about three feet from it when it started beating its wings together, rolling this way and that and rustling the long grass that surrounded it. Making a terrible noise, so loud that it alerted the still waiting keeper, looking back. The keeper must have known that there was a live bird caught and left it to give the alarm. It certainly worked, a loud shout went up and the keeper and friend, who I hadn't notice earlier, were headed my way, and fast.

I quickly gathered the birds I had, and made for the nearest wood, beating my way right into the heart of the thick wood and surrounded by a track. Then sat down and waited for the fun to start. My heart was pounding along with my head. But I sat tight, listening to see what was happening. I could hear a lot of discussion about which way I had gone and from what I could hear neighbour was right. They went up and down, keeping it up for about an hour before it was safe enough for me to leave the wood and go home.

Experience of my own and other people has taught us that when you become the hunted at night, head for a good size wood, as it is very unlikely that you will be found as long as you keep still and under cover.

That particular night I arrived home none the worse for my experience, apart form a few scratches to my face. Only to find that I now had six pheasants. I must have dropped one along the way. Now I wonder where that was, I thought. Mind you, I didn't fancy going back for it!

The Fox That Fought Back

Another frantic phone call from a lady who lives not too far from my home, was received one evening after work. This lady – 'Sue' by name, seems to live for nothing more than her family and animals. Over the years that I have known her she has kept just about every kind of animal that one could think of, or that the average smallholder could only dream of.

The most precious of her stock being her goats and chickens. Her goats are kept for the very good healthy milk that they supply. At my last visit I counted no less than six and all good milkers. The by-products of all the milk are of course cheese and yoghurt. All of which seem to be more popular by the day. She appears to sell all that she produces and I believe gets paid handsomely for her efforts. The other use that goats can be kept for, is meat personally having sampled a small amount of this, I must admit it isn't for me. However, many people adore the taste. Discussing the subject of slaughtering and eating young goats with Sue, is to say the least, interesting.

She knows the man who will do the deed, she knows how to butcher one and she knows how much each joint of meat will cost. But what is very mysterious is that I don't know of anyone who has actually witnessed her doing this. I am not sure if she had ever had a goat slaughtered for meat. But it's my opinion that she hasn't. I do believe it's just a front to cover up and of course, it makes her sound to others like the most up together smallholder for miles around.

Her chickens are another of her great loves. She owns all sorts. Pretty ones, ugly ones, and plain ones, and among them live her so called best ones. These consist of her prize winners. Sue enters quite a lot in Mainland shows and also local ones. She seems to do very well and has endless amounts of prizes and rosettes. But alas, it was to be no more. A hungry fox had somehow managed to enter the chicken house where it stole, killed and maimed all but a few of the birds. Sue was devastated, hence the phone call. She was fast after revenge by having the fox shot and wondered if I would help. Of course I would, I told her, and left home immediately to see for myself the devastation caused by the night visitor.

On my arrival Sue was stood by the front door. As I spoke to her it was easy to tell just how upset she was and not very far from tears. On going to inspect the ravage that the fox had left, it was very easy to see why she was so upset. All her best prize birds were dead. In fact, every bird that slept in that particular house had been killed. So I set about the task of putting paid to this cruel animal that had caused so much trouble.

One has to be licenced to obtain poisons for dealing with such pests these days, and as I was not, the idea of getting him that way was out of the question. So that left shooting or snaring him. I decided on the former. Although this can sometimes be a very long job and involves a great deal of standing around waiting for the fox to turn up, and this certainly was the case here. I made visits every night for abut a fortnight, but no sign whatsoever of the fox. The bait, in the form of some of the dead chickens, had not been touched, deciding to give it one more night's watching and waiting before giving up and calling it a day.

Arriving at Sue's once more, in plenty of time to make myself comfortable and settle in for another long wait. As the hours slowly rolled by my mind began to wander as it sometimes does on these occasions, back to my hunting trips as a young lad and sometimes the fishing that I have done in the past. If I think very hard, it is almost possible to relive the situation again. The funny thing is, that I always catch more thinking about it than I did on the actual night. There must be a message there somewhere, perhaps in not hunting properly.

My dreaming was suddenly disturbed by the sound of something biting into the carefully placed chicken carcass and on the large lawn in front of me. I could just make out the silhouette of a fox, tearing at the flesh on the bird All that remained for me to do was to take aim and fire. I was situated on the top of an old shed, which had a tin roof, so a great deal of care was needed in not making any noise when getting myself ready.

The weapon I was using was an old single barrel twelve bore, which I had had for quite a few years. It was very reliable and ideal for this sort of work. Slowly – I took aim, the fox was still busy feeding and quite oblivious to the fact that I was watching him. Just for a second or two he lifted his head and had a look around. For a moment there I thought he had detected me, but no, down went his head and he carried on feeding.

My sights were now on him, the trigger was pulled, a loud bang which seemed to echo for miles and miles, rang out and my job was done. The fox had been cleanly shot and was dead. I cleaned up before I felt and disposed of the chicken remans and the fox carcass, and went on my way. Deciding as I went, that it was quite a good night to be out. The fact that I had with me the lamp that I use for rabbiting. I took the long way home, crossing the fields and shining my lamp as I went. The beam of light shone over Wootton Creek, the light glistened on the still water. The land I stood on was quite high, so I had a good view up and down the valley. It was just light enough to make out the rooftops of houses. In the distance lights were being switched on as people began to rise after their night's sleep. How lucky they were I thought: What remained of the night was very still there was no wind or breeze at all. It sure was beautiful.

On I walked, homeward bound. I still had my lamp on, although it was hardly necessary. But just then I spotted another fox. He also had spotted me and was looking directly at me with those large saucer-like sharp eyes. I decided to try and get nearer to him in the hope that I might get near enough for anther shot. The land that I was now on belongs to very good friends of mine, who allow me to hunt on the land. They too have had their share of fox trouble and would welcome any chance of thinning out the fox population. Luck seemed to be with me that night. As I slowly got nearer and nearer to the fox, he just stood motionless watching me approach, and was soon within firing range. I no longer needed the beam of light from my lamp to aid me as I could see him very clearly. Then again, I took aim and again anther shot rang out and travelled down along the creek. The fox ran from where he had stood. I felt sure I had hit him. But on he went, I watched in disbelief. Then, all of a sudden, he dropped. Thank goodness for that, I thought, it would have been terrible if he had been wounded and got away only to die slowly in some undergrowth somewhere.

I casually walked up to the now still body of the fox, looking down at him I felt very guilty for my night's work. These animals really are beautiful, such a shame they have such destructive habits. Bending down I grabbed hold of his long brush in order to dispose of his body, when all of a sudden, the fox gave a quick movement and sunk his teeth into the upper part of my boot. The surprise of this was so severe that I let out an ear-piercing scream which in turn, like the reports from my gun, echoed down and along Wootton Creek and far off into the distance. It was terrifying to feel the animal's teeth holding my leg fast. Frantically I shook my leg, trying to shake him off. The noises that he was making reminded me of some kind of demon, he wouldn't let go and just held fast. I tried pulling him off with my hands, but to no avail. The only other option I could think of at the time, was to hit him with my gun, still no success. He seemed to hold even tighter, repeating my actions again and again. Thankfully he eventually let go, after me becoming what can only be described as frenzied. The fox once again laid motionless on the grass and scattered around him were bits of wood, springs and metal. All of this, I very soon recognised as parts of my gun. All that was left in my hand was the barrel and that was bent. After recovering and counting my losses, I collect my senses and quickly made my way home.

Early the next morning I reported to Sue, that I had put an end to the fox that had caused her so much trouble ad put her mind at rest. She has now rebuilt her stock that she lost, since then she has called me back twice to deal with more foxes. Luckily, I managed to shoot both offending beasts. But by now we must be due for another.

Ferreting for Beginners

As a youngster I was very fortunate in the fact that it was very easy to earn a shilling or two's pocket money in our area. There were various ways that my mates and I achieved this. One of my best memories of earning a bob or two was to go beating in the season for the local shoot. The pay was reasonable for a day's work and I might add was well earned. I remember it being a long hard day, walking mile after mile, over endless amounts of ploughed fields and through very thick undergrowth.

There were always a lot of my mates at such meetings, it seemed at the time that all our conversation consisted of was what mischief we could get up to next. The Gamekeeper in charge of the shoot was at that time, my Idol. I would eavesdrop on the conversation taking place between him and the men that had also come along for a day's beating or shooting. Most of the talk was about poachers that he had caught in the week, or deer which he had taken from the herds that were casing so much damage to newly planted forestry. Or what he and the Lord of the Estate had tot up to on previous hunting trips. I remember being so very impressed by all that happened and looking back now I feel sure that those first Saturday Beating trips were the ones that planted the hunting seed firmly in my head.

By beating on the Estate, one very soon learn where all the tracks and footpaths came from and went to. Where the pheasant pens were, and where the keeper lived. All essential bits of knowledge to a potential poacher.

We would pay quite a few trips to the Estate land in our hours of boredom during the school holidays. On one occasion we et up with one of the farm hand's son. He was about our age and very gullible. We managed to enter his father's garden shed, with the aid of a long metal bar, and help ourselves to his father's best ferret and about half a dozen rabbit wires. We soon set off in pursuit of our quarry. We hunted for hours with the ferret, practically putting him down every hole we could find. We were really wasting our time, as we forgot to take any purse nets with us. After a good day's walking we decided to call it a day. But vowed to return the day after.

At nine o'clock sharp the following day, we all met up once more and were soon on our way to the Estate grounds on which we had had so much fun the day before. This time we were fully equipped with ferrets, nets and rabbit snares. There would be no stopping us now. Again, we entered the ferrets down every available hole that could be seen. I can still remember thinking what an exciting way to spend my spare time.

We worked the ferrets for some time and did have some success with them. As I remember we caught five rabbits and were more than happy with our catch. The conversation that we all had was very young and boyish. Looking back, it was very amusing, it consisted of what we intended to do as a profession when we eventually left school. One of the answers were a gamekeeper of course. A professional poacher was another answer. A tracker of wild animals and the farm hand's son came up with nothing better than a tractor driver. We went on our way deeper into a wood to find more holes. But by now the novelty of ferreting was wearing off fast. We still had the rabbit snares with us and decided to give them a go.

We stared setting them along a nice straight wire fence, on ground where the grass was fairly long and it was easy to see where the rabbits were going to and from. We carried on setting a wire every now and then, in the hope of actually catching a rabbit by this method. As I suddenly glanced upwards, I could see a man standing watching us from abut five feet away. He was about five feet six inches in height, stockily built, deerstalker hat, plus fours, with a nice pair of shiny shoes. This man I knew very well – the Gamekeeper….

'Now then,' he said. 'What do you think you're up to?'

I soon nominated myself as spokesman, as it didn't seem that anyone else was going to and I replied –

'We're only having a go at setting some rabbit wires Charlie. We didn't think we were doing any harm.'

'You're not doing any harm,' he said. 'But you're not allowed over here and you know it, don't you? Been doing some ferreting as well, I see,' he said, looking at the ferret box and the rabbits.

Then all of a sudden, he lunged forward and opened the ferret box, with near screams he said 'Where the bloody hell did you come by these?' referring to the ferrets.

All eyes went immediately towards Stephen, the farm hand's son.

'He gave them to us,' we said.

'Yes,' said the Gamekeeper, 'and I was the one who gave them to his Dad.'

He then went on about his rights and wrongs of hunting, on someone else's land without permission, he took all our names. The farm hand's son of course he already knew, he was sent on home by the gamekeeper and was told to tell his Dad that he would be around to see him later that evening.

Then he told the rest of us to be on our way home, 'and before you go,' he said, 'who was the one who set these wires?'

'It was me,' I replied.

'Well they're not set right,' he said. 'Ere, let me show you how it's done.' He then proceeded to kneel down before our very eyes and demonstrate the correct way to set a rabbit wire. A lesson I have never forgotten and one I have found most useful over the years!

A Close Shave

For quite a few weeks, a young lad who was showing a slight interest in the sport of lamping, had been pestering me for a night's hunting. As a rule, I am apprehensive of taking young lads with me, as I find they have loose tongues and tend to brag about the night's events.

However, I finally gave in and invited him along. Arrangements were made as to where and when to pick him up. Eight o'clock that evening we met. I became increasingly worried as we drove along the road, as he never stopped talking about the forthcoming events. He was really excited about it all.

When eventually I managed to stop his endless chat, I filled him in on a few details which I thought might be of interest to him. Like, which way to run, what to say if you get caught, (which is easy – nothing) and which was the safest way home. He seemed to have taken in all that I had said, then I went on to tell him what we were hunting, and how many we were after, i.e. rabbits and hares.

We were not far from approaching our destination. We parked the van and started to walk our first field and within a few minutes put up our first hare of the evening. The course was a good one. The hare and dogs went up and down. Unfortunately, the hare had a very good escape route, and took it at the first available opportunity. I spotted a rabbit sat way out on a newly sown field and this was our next course. Very short though it was. The rabbit was caught by Belle and retrieved to hand.

My new partner for the night informed me that he was absolutely astounded by what he had just seen. 'That's nothing,' I replied, 'there's more to come.' I understood exactly how he felt as I had the same feelings when I saw a dog catch a rabbit for the first time.

Not long after we found the second of the two hares I had spotted earlier. Off he ran, he seemed to be alerted long before we got to him, so he was given such a good start I decided to leave him for another day. We were both just squeezing through a little gap in the hedge when my mate tapped me on the shoulder, 'What does he want now?' I thought.

'Is this bloke a mate of yours?' he said.

'What bloke?' I asked, looking around, and there to my horror was a large figure of a man with a strong torch, not ten feet from us.

My heart fell all the way to my feet, and landed with a thud. 'Run!' I said.

We ran over the field, the ground was heavy, as we had had a lot of rain recently and the field was newly sown. We finally got across it and came to the next fence, experience of getting through fences made it easy for me, my mate however appeared to be in deep shock. Fumbling about and making a compete mess of getting through the fence, finally getting well and truly stuck, as the barbed wire held him tight. Taking a quick look up the field, I could see the man still coming with torch blazing and heading straight for us. I found myself starting to panic. Fighting desperately with the sharp wire that was keeping my mate captive. After a long struggle he was free and not before time, the man still in hot pursuit was now about twenty feet from us. Our advantage was that we were the other side of the fence. We ran off again, covering a lot of ground in a short time and the man finally gave up the chase. We relaxed and made our way slowly back to the van. As I drove my mate back to his house, it dawned on me, he hadn't said a word since our little run. Funny what a bit of exercise can do for the tongue!

And so, I come to the end of my Book –

I have tried to give the reader some idea of the fun I have had in the countryside over the past years. I have thoroughly enjoyed meeting people with the same interests as myself. When it was first suggested that I sat down and put pen to paper on my subject, I felt very unsure that it could be done. As I have done but a very small part of what others may have done. But to my family it has been good fun reminiscing over events in the past and present.

To my mother and father especially, it has been quite an eye opener. They say that they never knew so much was going on behind their backs. To quote what has now become a popular phrase of my mother: 'It make me go cold when I think of the trouble you could have got yourself into!'

My wife, whose name should be 'Patience', or perhaps 'Forgiving', has stood by my side and given me rope enough to do more or less what I want with hunting (although she doesn't agree to it). But she has never been slow to pull the said 'rope' in tightly when she feels I have gone too far. She has sat night after night and hour after hour when I have been out hunting with the dogs, wondering what time I would be back, or even if I would be back. Wondering if I have come too close to a Gamekeeper or Water Bailiff and has always celebrated with me on a good night's hunting.

On many occasions I have said to my wife, 'I won't be long, about an hour. Just going to give the dogs a quick run,' and then not returned home four or five hours later. I have searched my brain for excuses for being late – just before getting home.

On one instance I opened the door and there she was, stood like a stone, waiting for my excuse, (any lamper will know the look she gave me). Quickly thinking I said 'Why didn't you pay the ransom money? I've been held hostage in a house in the woods.'

The stone straight face, became a grin and once again I was forgiven. Yes, a truly marvellous wife I have, who spoils me rotten.

One other person I would like to mention is the man responsible for introducing me to the noble lurcher dog.

'Get one of these dogs,' he said, 'and every other form of hunting will be boring.'

How right he was.

Since the first time I saw this man's dog course and catch a rabbit, we struck up a very good friendship. I look on him as the man who has the most skills with running dogs, and if I have problems or queries to be answered, he is the man to see.

Thanks to Mervin I have found freedom in my spare time, excitement and companionship with my lovely dogs.

A Last Note

I felt it quite necessary to write about various events in my younger days, such as how I passed my spare time and how I would earn my pocket money, because I believe it was those early days that have moulded me into what I am today. There are many people I have met that try very hard to do the same as myself with our outdoor life, but one usually finds that they very soon give up and fade away into the background. You see an outdoor man or boy, or someone who likes to study the ways of animals and plants and be in their company, isn't made, they are born. Especially with the hunting. It goes back thousands of years to when man had to hunt to stay alive. As time has passed the instinct in most of us has all but disappeared. My estimate, taken from a personal survey, is that one person in fifty still retains this instinct good and strong. I really am glad to say, I am one of the few.

I have enjoyed every hunting trip and countryside outing that I have ever been on, to the full. No matter how small. Each time I have learnt something new. If I live to be a hundred, I will still be learning. In my everyday life I find things like studying and learning new ways to do things at work or, perhaps, at home, very difficult. But to be questioned about dogs, birds of prey, or wildlife in general, these things I find surprisingly easy to answer, and to pass on any knowledge to anyone who is interested.

I consider that I have been gifted with the fact that I am able to learn so easily, the things that are natural to man, and thank the Lord that I am so happy with it.

Printed in Great Britain
by Amazon